Get Ready for Squash

GET READY FOR SQUASH

A COMPLETE TRAINING PROGRAMME

David Collins
Claire Chapman
Anne de Looy
Peter Thomas

The Crowood Press

First published in 1990 by
The Crowood Press
Gipsy Lane
Swindon
Wiltshire SN2 6DQ

British Library Cataloguing in Publication Data

Get ready for squash.
   1. Squash rackets
   I. Collins, David
   796.343

ISBN 1 85223 389 3

Line-drawings by Jan Sparrow
Photographs by Allsport

Throughout this book the pronouns 'he', 'him' and 'his' have been used inclusively, and are intended to apply to both men and women. It is important in sport, as elsewhere, that women and men should have equal status and equal opportunities.

Typeset by PCS Typesetting, Frome, Somerset BA11 1EB.
Printed and bound in Great Britain by
Dotesios Printers Ltd, Trowbridge, Wiltshire.

Contents

THE AUTHORS

DAVID COLLINS: David is Senior Lecturer in movement studies at St Mary's College, Twickenham. He studied sport psychology at Pennsylvania State University, USA and has acted as a consultant in this field at all levels of sports and athletics. David is a qualified British Amateur Weight Lifters' Association coach and is a staff tutor for the National Coaching Foundation.

Dr PETER THOMAS: Peter is a sports physician and was an Olympic oarsman in the Mexico games of 1968. He is now the Great Britain rowing team doctor, medical director of Reading Sports Injury Clinic and Lecturer on the London Hospital diploma course in sports medicine. He is staff tutor to the National Coaching Foundation.

Dr ANNE DE LOOY: Anne is Principal Lecturer in nutrition and dietetics at Leeds Polytechnic and is a consultant to the National Coaching Foundation on sports nutrition. She also has an active interest and involvement in cycling, rhythmic gymnastics and swimming.

CLAIRE CHAPMAN: Claire is the Squash Rackets Association National Coaching and Development Manager based in London. From 1976–80 she coached and managed the British women's squash team and from 1976–84 the England 'B' squad. Claire has also played for the British squash team between 1962–71 and pursues her interest in squash at every opportunity.

Introduction

Since the sudden increase in the popularity of squash in the 1970s, it has maintained its position as one of the UK's most popular indoor sports. Easier access to courts, both public and private, has helped to ensure that the game is played by a wide cross-section of the community, with an equally wide variation in skill level and commitment. Whatever your ability level or your desire to succeed, any extra knowledge about the game cannot help but increase your enjoyment and standard of play. This book aims to provide that knowledge and it is presented for you in an easily digestible format. In addition, unlike other coaching texts, the book covers all the major aspects of a player's performance at one go. Apart from the obvious chapter on skill development, advice is offered on mental and physical training, nutrition and the prevention and basic treatment of injury. All the information within each topic is related specifically to squash. This comprehensive approach should provide you with all the facts necessary to improve your game, whatever your starting point or ambition.

1   Skills Practices

One of the many assets of squash as a game is that, being a wall game, the skills can be practised by one player. With a partner of similar standard it becomes possible to use and practise realistic shot sequences that happen in the game. Bring in a third player and extra pressure can be put on one player to move more quickly to the ball.

Most shot sequences can be used to practise more than one shot and some of the most useful and popular ones are illustrated. Once these basic routines have been understood and practised, the variations can easily be grasped. Many of the sequences can be played as a game by defining the area in which the shots must land and scoring points for each rally won.

By giving one or both players the option of two or three possible shots the sequence becomes unpredictable, so improving a player's anticipation and stopping him from being too rigidly programmed in his game. In the text and diagrams, both players are seen as right-handers. All practices should be played on forehand and backhand sides with both players returning to the T between shots. (*See* Diagram A.) The most important teaching points and practices are given for the six basic shots – DRIVE – VOLLEY – SERVICE – BOAST – DROP – LOB.

DRIVES

More than half the shots played in a rally will be straight and cross-court drives and players of any standard can and should aim to improve the length and width of this shot.

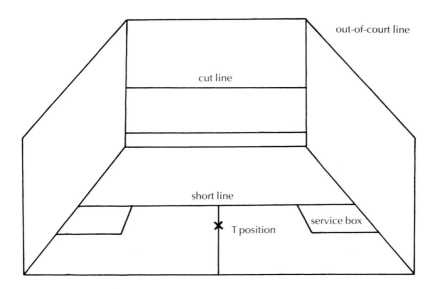

Diagram A

The straight shot must travel close to the side wall, as well as taking its second bounce near the back wall, to be really effective in the game. The target areas for drives are shown in Diagram B.

The following points will help to achieve a consistent quality shot.

Coaching Points

(i)   All shots in squash are played with a 'shake hands' grip which keeps the racket face open.

(ii)   Take up a sideways position with shoulders facing the side wall for the straight shot and facing the front corner for the cross-court shot.

(iii)   Hit at a comfortable distance opposite the leading leg for the forehand straight drive and slightly further forward for the backhand drive. The cross-court drive is hit earlier.

(iv)   The swing is a throwing action, taking the racket high and following through high. Backswing needs to be early to give time for the shot and should start as the opponent's shot hits the front wall.

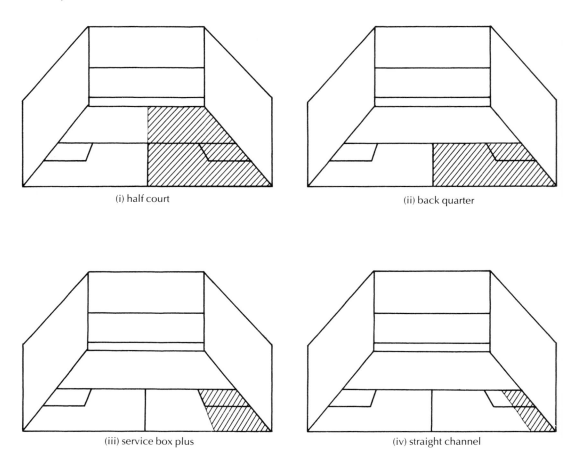

(i) half court

(ii) back quarter

(iii) service box plus

(iv) straight channel

Diagram B (i)–(iv)

Straight Length

Solo Practices

(1)   Play a rally of consecutive drives which all bounce behind the short line. As accuracy improves the target area can be reduced so that all the shots land in the service box or into a thin corridor chalked on the floor.

(2)   Play a rally of consecutive drives, hitting the front wall alternately above and below the cut line.

(3)   Long, long, short rally. Hit two length drives and one short shot, bringing in movement up and down the court.

(4)   Overhit drives. Rally of consecutive drives played to hit the back wall first and high enough so that they can be hit after bouncing on the floor.

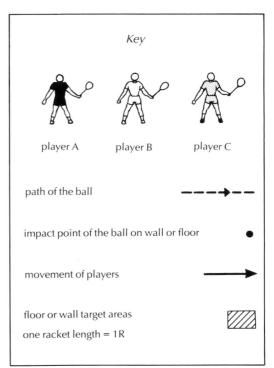

Key

player A   player B   player C

path of the ball   ---->--

impact point of the ball on wall or floor   ●

movement of players   ⟶

floor or wall target areas   ▨

one racket length = 1R

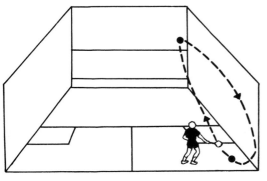

Drill 4

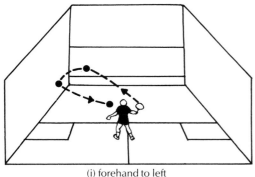

(i) forehand to left

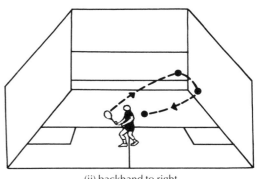

(ii) backhand to right

Drill 5 (i) and (ii)

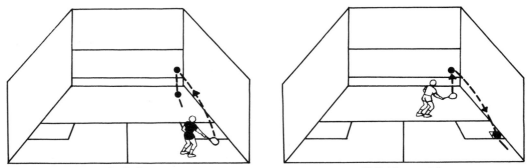

(i) A feeds short

(ii) B drives straight

Drill 6 (i) and (ii)

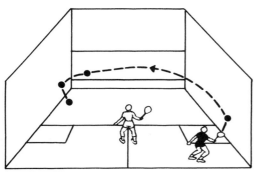

(i) A boasts

(ii) B drives

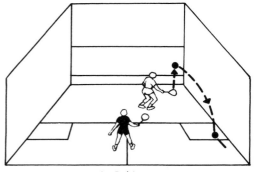

(iii) A boasts

(iv) B drives

Drill 11 (i)–(iv)

(5) Figure eight rally. Standing in mid-court, play the ball alternately forehand and backhand to hit first the left-hand and then the right-hand front corner (*see* page 11).

Pairs Practices

(6) Target drives. A sets up a short straight shot which bounces a few feet from the front wall. B aims to hit a perfect straight length. The ball should return close to the side wall and bounce for the second time near the back wall. A piece of card placed in the back corner of the service box makes a useful target for the first bounce.

(7) Straight rally. Both players try to maintain a continuous rally with every shot aimed to land in the same half (side) of the court. As the skill improves, the target can be made smaller.

(8) Straight rally to back quarter. Both players try to play every shot into the same side of the court and behind the short line.

(9) Straight rally to the service box. Both players rally into the service box.

(10) Straight corridor rally. Both players

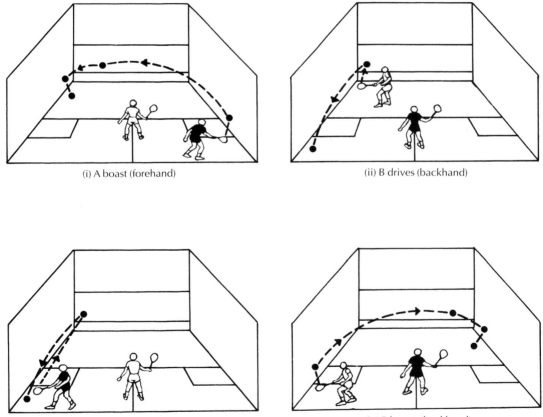

(i) A boast (forehand)

(ii) B drives (backhand)

(iii) A drives (backhand)

(iv) B boasts (backhand)

Drill 13 (i)–(vi)

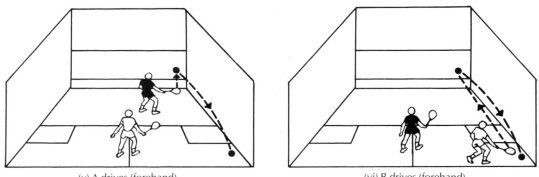

(v) A drives (forehand)

(vi) B drives (forehand)

Drill 13 continued

(i) A feeds short ball

(ii) B drives straight

(iii) C feeds short ball

(iv) B drives straight

Drill 17 (i)–(iv)

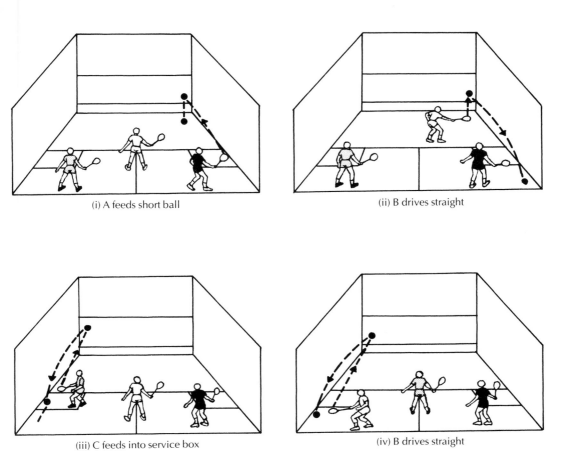

(i) A feeds short ball

(ii) B drives straight

(iii) C feeds into service box

(iv) B drives straight

Drill 20 (i)–(iv)

rally finally into a corridor marked with a chalk line half the width of the service box or less.

(11) Boast and drive. A boasts on the forehand, B returns this shot from the opposite front corner as a backhand straight drive. A returns this shot as a boast on the backhand, B plays a forehand straight drive and the sequence continues until one player fails to return the ball (*see* page 12).

(12) Boast and drive game. Use the sequence from drill 11 and play a game with a point scored every time a player fails to return a shot into the target area.

(13) Boast and two drives. Adding a second straight drive to the sequence from drill 12 makes each player hit one drive from the front of the court and one from the back and brings in far more movement (*see* page 13).

(14) Boast and three drives. Bringing in a third drive makes one player move a great deal in order to play a drive from the front and a drive from the back on each side.

(15) Short and long. A plays any short ball (straight or cross-court drop, or boast), B returns a straight drive along the nearest side wall.

(16) Short and long game. Scoring the rallies

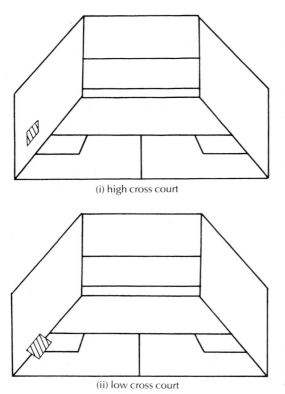

(i) high cross court

(ii) low cross court

Diagram C (i) and (ii)

and setting targets for the drive of drill 15 makes this a very demanding exercise for the player hitting drives.

Practices for Three

(17)   Alternate drives – target time. With a ball each, A and C take turns to set up a short shot (either with a throw or a short racket feed), for the third player B to hit a straight drive. B must return to the T between shots. Set a time for B to hit as many shots as possible into the defined target area.

(18)   Alternate shots – target shots. Using the same format as drill 17, the player has to achieve a set number of shots into the target area.

(19)   Alternate shots – target/time. A varia-tion of drill 18 is for the player to be timed try-ing to hit as many shots as possible into the target area.

(20)   Drive from front and back. Again using two balls, A sets up (feeds) a short ball for B to drive. C feeds a longer ball which B has to drive from near the back of the service box. To avoid collisions between B and C, player C must feed the longer shot from slightly further up the court and then move towards the T to allow B to return the shot (*see* page 20).

Cross-court Length

The length and width of the cross-court shot may be varied according to the opponent's position but is most often played to hit the side wall low, just behind the back line of the service box. The target areas for cross-court shots are shown in Diagram C.

Solo Practices

(21)   Play a rally of alternate straight and cross-court drives.

Pairs Practices

(22)   Boast and cross-court drive. A boasts and B returns a cross-court drive. Both players should return to the T between shots.

(23)   Cross-court game. Both players hit cross-court drives to each other.

(24)   Cross-court game – racket target. Standing a racket up against the side wall just behind each service box makes this more fun as the players can score points each time they succeed in knocking it over.

(25)   Boast, cross court, straight. A boasts, B drives cross court, A drives straight and so on. This three-shot sequence occurs very fre-quently in the game in various forms. The cross-court shot may be either a drive, a lob or the service and the straight length may be played either as a drive or a volley.

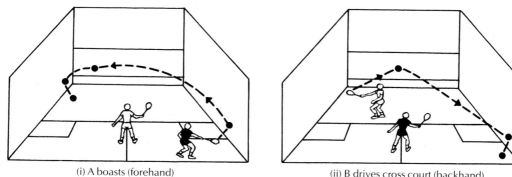

(i) A boasts (forehand)

(ii) B drives cross court (backhand)

Drill 22 (i) and (ii)

(i) A boasts

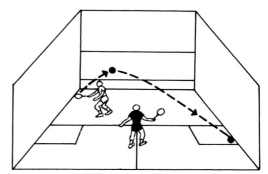

(ii) B drives cross court

(iii) A drives straight

Drill 25 (i)–(iii)

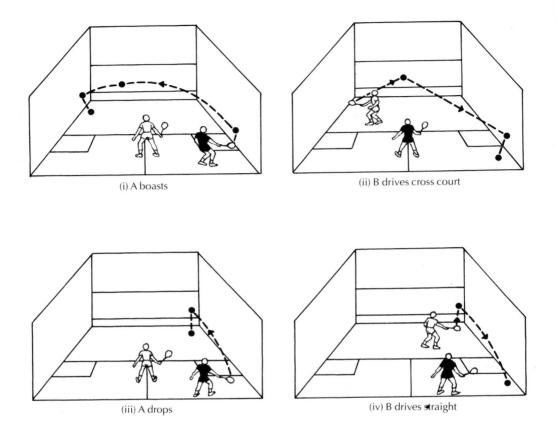

(i) A boasts

(ii) B drives cross court

(iii) A drops

(iv) B drives straight

Drill 28 (i)–(iv)

(26) Boast, cross court and two straight. Adding a second straight length to the sequence keeps one player relatively stationary while the other player has to cover a great deal of ground to play the cross-court drive from the front and the straight drive from the back.

(27) Boast, cross court, straight drive/boast. Giving the player of the straight drive an option to boast so that the sequence becomes unpredictable is a further variation.

(28) Short and long. A boasts, B drives cross court, A drops, B drives straight. In this sequence too, only one player is moving and playing alternate straight and cross-court drives.

(29) Short (varied) and long. A has the option of playing either a boast or a drop, making the sequence unpredictable for B, who has to return the shots to A's side of the court with straight and cross-court drives.

(30) Short and long (varied). An option can also be given to B to choose the straight or the cross-court shot.

(31) Short and long with volley. The drop can be replaced with a high straight shot, so that B has to volley straight.

(32) Short and long game. Once players can keep these rallies going for six or more shots, they can be played as a game. The rally is lost if the length drive fails to hit a target area or the short shot fails to reach the front wall.

Practice Games

(33)   One player plays only straight shots – short or long, hard or soft and only boasts if the ball cannot be returned any other way.

(34)   One player plays only straight length shots, so that the point is lost if the ball bounces in front of the short line or on the wrong side of the court. With increasing accuracy, the player should only use the width of the service box.

(35)   One player may play only length shots, straight or cross court.

(36)   Both players play only lengths, in half the court (side).

(37)   Both players play only length in the width of the service box.

(38)   Three-quarter court game. Players may use three-quarters of the court with one back quarter used only as an area to serve from.

VOLLEYS

A sound volley is essential for the squash player as it may be the only way to return a good length high serve or lob. The volley has the added advantage of cutting the ball off early, giving the opponent less time. Depending on the tactical situation, the volley may be played as a length or a short shot and either straight, cross court or angled (volley boast). Note: the targets for length volleys are the same as those shown for drives, in Diagram B.

Accuracy is vital and the following points should help.

Length Volleys

Coaching Points

(i)   Use the same sideways position as for the drive, with good balance throughout the shot.

(ii)   Hit it higher and early, slightly ahead of the leading shoulder.

(iii)   Try for a punchy action with the wrist kept firm and the racket head above the hand.

Solo Practices

(39)   Practise a rally of consecutive volleys, played close to the wall.

(40)   Play a rally of consecutive volleys starting close to the wall and moving one pace back every six shots until the back line of the service box is reached. Then move forward, still maintaining the rally, until the starting position is regained.

(41)   Short-line rally. Start a forehand rally standing in the right-hand service box and moving gradually backwards along the short line until the left-hand service box is reached. Turn and move back to the starting position playing backhand volleys.

(42)   Play a corner rally of consecutive volleys into one front corner, playing alternate forehand and backhand shots to hit the front wall, side wall and then the side wall, front wall (*see* page 20).

(43)   Figure eight rally. Practise as in drill 5 but use volleys in place of drives.

Pairs Practices

(44)   Drive – volley. A sets up (feeds) a short straight shot, B drives straight, A feeds a high straight shot, B volleys straight to length (*see* page 20).

(45)   Volley rally. Both players rally down the side wall, volleying lengths close to the side wall and trying to keep in front of their partner (*see* page 21).

(46)   Boast, cross-court lob, straight volley. This is essentially the same as drill 25, with the cross-court shot played high and the straight shot as a volley.

(47)   Alternate straight volleys. A feeds alternate straight and cross-court high shots, B volleys straight (*see* page 22).

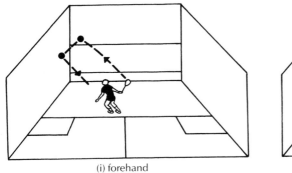 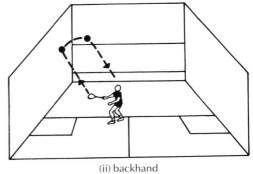

| (i) forehand | (ii) backhand |

Drill 42 (i) and (ii)

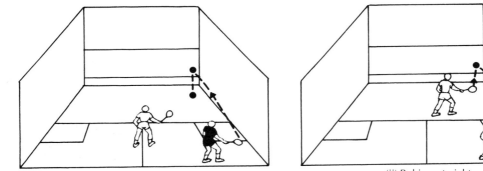

| (i) A feeds short, low shot | (ii) B drives straight |

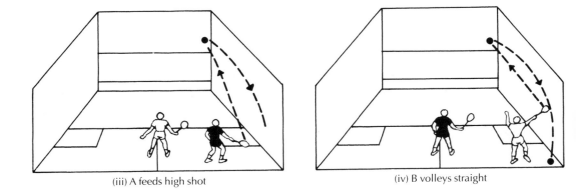

| (iii) A feeds high shot | (iv) B volleys straight |

Drill 44 (i)–(iv)

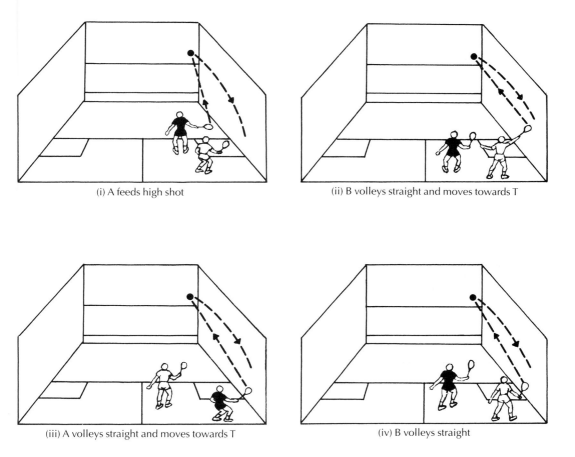

(i) A feeds high shot

(ii) B volleys straight and moves towards T

(iii) A volleys straight and moves towards T

(iv) B volleys straight

Drill 45 (i)–(iv)

(48) Alternate straight volleys (variable feed). Allowing A to feed either a straight or a cross-court shot makes this a more demanding practice for B.

(49) Straight and cross-court volleys. A feeds a straight high shot. B volleys either straight or cross court.

(50) Straight and cross-court volleys – variable feed. The practice can be made more demanding by giving A the option of feeding straight or cross court.

(51) Length volley game. This practice can be scored as a game where B scores a point if A's return hits the floor in front of the short line and A scores if his shot hits the back wall.

Practices for Three

(52) Alternate straight volleys. The same set up as drill 17, but the two feeders set up high straight shots for B to volley straight.

Short Volleys and Volley Boast

All these short volleys need to hit the floor as close as possible to the front wall. The straight shot should be aimed to hit the front wall low and very close to the side wall. The cross-court shot is aimed to hit the front wall low and then the nick, or at least hit the side wall very low. The volley boast is aimed to hit the nearest side wall, the front wall and either the opposite side wall low or bounce for the second time before it reaches the side wall.

Coaching Point

(i)   The short volleys are easier to control if a fair amount of cut is applied to the ball, to bring it sharply downwards and reduce the pace. The target areas for short volleys are shown in Diagram D.

Solo Practices

(53)   Short volleys. Set up a high shot and volley it short to a target area on the floor at the front of the court.

Pairs Practices

(54)   Short volley and drive. A feeds a high straight shot, B plays a short straight volley and then drives his own shot back to A.
(55)   Short volley and lob. A lobs straight, B volleys short and straight.
(56)   Alternate straight volley. A lobs cross court, B volleys short and straight to alternate sides.

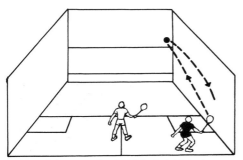

(i) A sets up (feeds) high straight shot

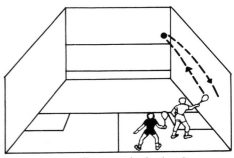

(ii) B volleys straight (forehand)

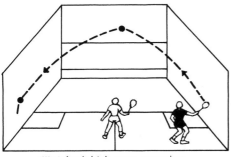

(iii) A feeds high cross-court shot

(iv) B volleys straight (backhand)

Drill 47 (i)–(iv)

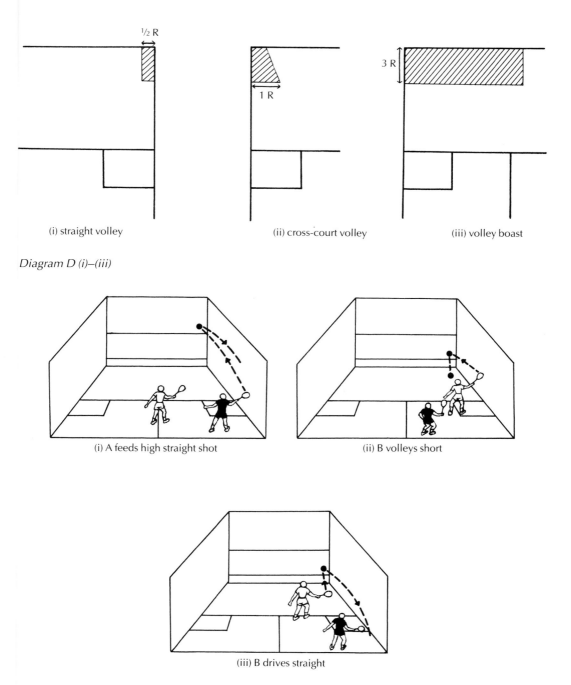

½ R

1 R

3 R

(i) straight volley

(ii) cross-court volley

(iii) volley boast

Diagram D (i)–(iii)

(i) A feeds high straight shot

(ii) B volleys short

(iii) B drives straight

Drill 54 (i)–(iii)

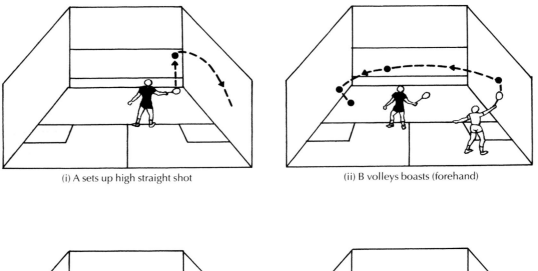

(i) A sets up high straight shot

(ii) B volleys boasts (forehand)

(iii) A lobs cross court (backhand)

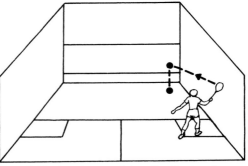

(iv) B plays short, straight volley (forehand)

Drill 61 (i)–(iv)

(57) Cross-court volleys. A lobs straight for B to volley short, cross court.

(58) Alternate straight and cross-court volley. A lobs straight, B volleys cross court, A lobs cross court, B volleys straight.

Practices for Three

(59) Alternate straight volleys. Use the same set-up as drill 17, but vary the play so that the two feeders set up high straight shots for B to volley short and straight. Another option is for B to volley short on one side and to length on the other.

(60) Long/short volley game. A feeds a consistent high straight shot. B can choose to play a straight length or short volley. Both length and short volleys have to be played to target areas and points can be scored and lost for hits and misses.

(61) Volley boast and straight. A feeds a medium-height straight shot, B volley boasts, A feeds a medium-height cross-court shot, B plays a short straight volley.

Note: in all the short volley practices where one player is lobbing from the front of the court for their partner to volley, the front court player must take care to keep out of the way by moving back between shots or the practice will be dangerous.

Most of the sequences including a boast can be modified to practice volley boasts if the previous shot is played as a high drive or a lob as shown in drills 62–5.

(62)   Boast and drive high. This is essentially the same as drill 11, but B hits a high shot for A to volley boast.

(63)   Boast, drive, drive (high), boast. Almost the same procedure as detailed in drill 13, but with the second drive played high to allow the player to volley boast.

(64)   Boast, cross court. Using the set-up of drill 22, but this time B hits a high cross-court drive for A to volley boast.

(65)   Boast, cross court (lob), straight. Similar to drill 25, but the cross-court shot is played as a high drive.

Practice Games

(66)   Volley game. Play a game scoring each rally up to ten points, players taking turns to serve. The volley must be aimed at the opposite back quarter of the court. The rally is lost if the ball is hit out, in the tin or the floor outside the opposite back quarter. Aiming the

volley to hit the side wall above head height at around the level of the back line of the service box makes it far more difficult to return.

(67)   Defending the back wall. Play a normal game, but with one player not allowing any shot to touch the back wall or he loses the rally.

(68)   In this game players score a bonus point if they win the rally with a volley or short volley.

(69)   Players can only win each rally of this game with a volley.

SERVICE

There are two types of basic serve, a high lob and a low hard shot. Both of these and the numerous variants can be used to try to force an error or at least a weak, defensive return from the opponent.

Service Rules

The rules of the game change every few years so it is important to keep up to date.

The latest rule changes of May 1989 alter the existing service rules and allow only **one serve**.

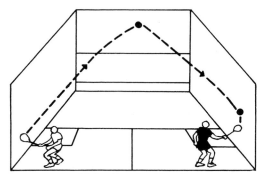

(i) A volleys (forehand)   (ii) B volleys (backhand)

Drill 66 (i) and (ii)

(i)   The server must have one foot on the floor inside the lines of the service box when the ball is struck.

(ii)   The serve must hit the front wall first and between the cut line and the out-of-court line.

(iii)   The ball must land (unless volleyed) inside the lines of the opposite back quarter.

Failure to comply with these rules is a service fault and the right to serve goes to the opponent. Unless the courts are very warm, service practice alone allows the ball to cool down and become much slower, bearing little resemblance to the ball a player will be serving with in a match. To overcome this problem, it is better to alternate a rally-type practice with the serve; as in drill 4, playing overhit drives.

The target areas for the service are shown in Diagram E.

Solo Practices

(70)   Lob serve to target. To be fully effective, this serve should rise higher than the out-of-court line but needs to be played with care as touching the line, the wall above it,

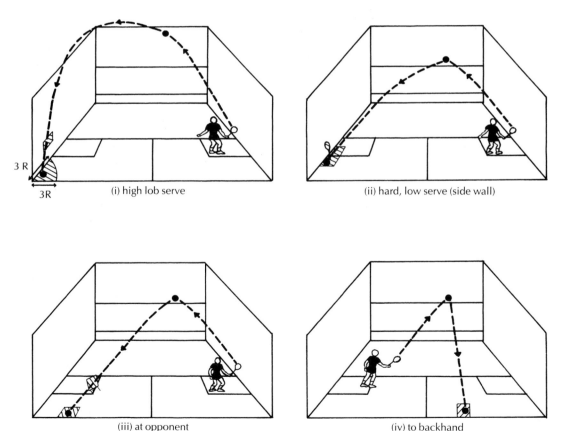

(i) high lob serve

3 R

3R

(ii) hard, low serve (side wall)

(iii) at opponent

(iv) to backhand

Diagram E (i)–(iv)

lights, beams or the ceiling results in loss of the serve.

The lob serve should drop to the floor near the back wall of the court and be aimed to hit the side wall at head height at around the level of the back line of the service box. This area can be marked with a sheet of paper fixed on the wall with Blutak.

(71) Low, hard serve to target. This is usually aimed to hit the side wall low near the back of the service box. A racket propped up against the side wall just behind the service box makes a good target for this serve.

For variations the target could be your opponent or his backhand side when serving from the left. Persuading a practice partner to act as a target may be difficult so a small easel could be a good substitute. Place it outside the back corner of the service box in the position usually occupied by the receiver.

Pairs Practices

Many of the practices, particularly the ones that use a cross-court shot can start off with a serve; for example, drill 25, the boast, cross court, straight.

(72) Target serves – competing with a partner for points. Score one point for a serve landing in the target area on the floor and score two points if it also hits the side wall where this is relevant. Score four points if the serve hits the target.

(73) Serve and return. A serves, B tries to play a straight length return and both players continue to alternate straight length shots until the rally breaks down.

Practices for Three

(74) Competing with your partner for points, have a third player standing in front of the short line on the receiver's side, trying to catch the ball. Should a catch be made, the server does not score.

Practice Games

(75) Play a normal game, but allow a second serve if the ball is out.

BOAST

The standard three-wall boast is aimed to hit the nearest side wall, the front wall fairly low and the opposite side wall very low. With practice and a little bit of luck, some of these will hit the nick and be unplayable.

The alternative two-wall boast is usually played as an attacking shot from in front of the opponent and is aimed to die after hitting the front wall low and before it reaches the opposite side wall. All boasts should hit the floor close to the front wall to be effective in the game. The target areas for boasts are shown in Diagram F.

Coaching Points

(i) The body position is much the same as for drives, but turned more towards the back corner as the boast is played from deeper in the court.

(ii) The ball is hit slightly later and up the side wall with an open racket face.

Solo Practices

(76) Rally down the side wall and choose a shot to boast, aiming for a target area.

(77) Boast, cross court. Playing a weak cross-court shot to return the boast brings in more movement. Continue the straight rally after the cross court.

Pairs Practices

Many of the practices already used for other shots include a boast and can be used to practise the shot.

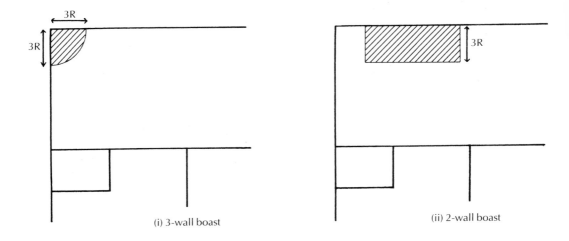

3R

3R

3R

(i) 3-wall boast

(ii) 2-wall boast

Diagram F (i) and (ii)

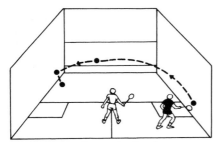

(i) A boasts (forehand)

(ii) B hits short cross court (backhand)

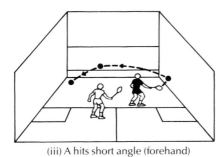

(iii) A hits short angle (forehand)

(iv) B hits long cross court (backhand)

Drill 78 (i)–(iv)

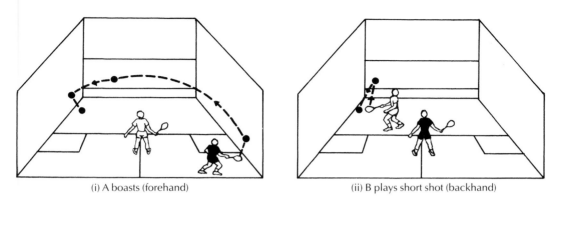

(i) A boasts (forehand)

(ii) B plays short shot (backhand)

(iii) A boasts (short angle, backhand)

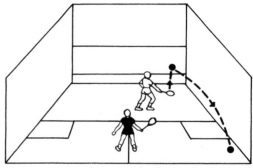

(iv) B drives straight (forehand)

Drill 79 (i)–(iv)

The most useful ones are:

(i) drill 11 – boast and straight drive;
(ii) drill 13 – boast and two straight drives;
(iii) drill 22 – boast and cross-court drive;
(iv) drill 25 – boast, cross-court, straight drive.

(78) Boast, cross court (long/short). A boasts, B hits a short cross-court shot, A boasts. (Note: this shot is probably better described as a short angle.) B hits cross-court length.
(79) Boast, drop, boast, drive. A boasts, B feeds a short, straight shot, A boasts (short angle), B drives straight. A variation of this sequence is to play a cross-court drive instead of the straight drive.
(80) Rally and boast. Both players rally down the side wall and can choose when to play the boast and so try to win the rally.

Practice Games

(81) One player may only straight drive or boast.
(82) One player must hit the side wall before the front wall on every shot.

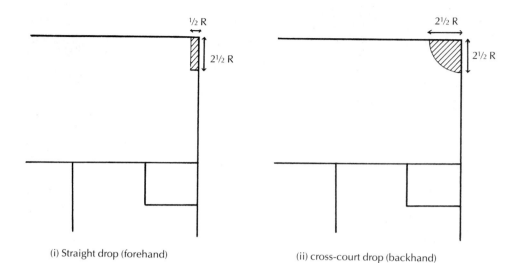

(i) Straight drop (forehand)   (ii) cross-court drop (backhand)

Diagram G (i) and (ii)

(83)   Players score a bonus point if they can win the rally with a boast.

DROP

The drop is aimed to hit the front wall just above the tin and drop short. The straight drop should cling to the side wall and the cross-court drop hit the front wall and then the side wall low, trying to hit the nick. The target areas for the drop are shown in Diagram G.

Coaching Points

(i)   Use the same sideways position as used for drives.
(ii)   It is important to bend the knees and keep a low, balanced position.
(iii)   Hit the ball slightly further ahead than for drives.
(iv)   Play a shorter, slower stroke with the racket face open to cut the ball and make it die more quickly.

Solo Practices

(84)   Target drops. Play a mid-length drive or a high boast and then a drop into the target area.
(85)   Play a rally of three or more drives, then play a drop.

Pairs Practices

(86)   Target drops. A feeds a short, straight shot, B drops straight. Variations on this are for B to:

(i)   drop cross court;
(ii)   choose to drop straight or cross court;
(iii)   vary the length of the feed so that the drop has to be played at different distances from the front wall;
(iv)   feed a short, cross-court shot;
(v)   the ultimate development is for A to feed any length straight or cross court and for B to play any short shot (drop or boast).

(87)   Boast and drop. A boasts, B drops

British Open Champion for nine consecutive years – Jahangir winding up for another powerful backhand.

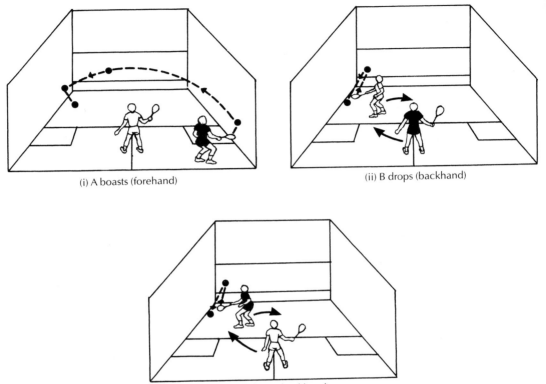

(i) A boasts (forehand)

(ii) B drops (backhand)

(iii) A drops (backhand)

Drill 87 (i)–(iii)

straight, A counter drops. The players then continue to alternate drop shots until the rally breaks down. To avoid collisions the players need to move away from the shot quickly, towards the centre of the court.

(88) Boast, drop, drive. A boasts, B drops straight, A drives straight. The same sequence can be played with a cross-court drop or a cross-court drive.

(89) An alternative way of playing the sequence of drill 88 is for B to hit two consecutive shots, returning his own drop shot with a drive. Take care that the drop is not played badly in order to ensure it is possible to return the ball.

(90) Long, long, short. A drives straight, B drives straight, A drops straight and so on.

(91) Boast, drop, drop, drive. A boasts, B feeds a short straight shot, A drops straight, B drives cross court. An alternative sequence is to use a straight drive (*see* page 35).

(92) Rally and drop. Players rally to length down the side wall and choose when to drop short, trying to win the rally.

Practices for Three

Drill 17 makes an excellent practice for drop shots. Players A and C each have a ball and feed with a gentle throw to the front wall. B drops on each side in turn. Emphasis must be placed on B to reposition at the T after each shot.

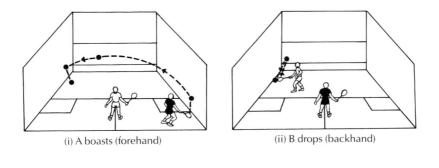

(i) A boasts (forehand)

(ii) B drops (backhand)

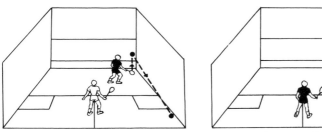

(iii) A drives straight (backhand)

Drill 88 (i)–(iii)

(i) A drives straight (forehand)

(ii) B drives straight (forehand)

(iii) A drops straight (forehand)

Drill 90 (i)–(iii)

The concentration of the squash player shown by World no. 1 Susan Devoy of New Zealand.

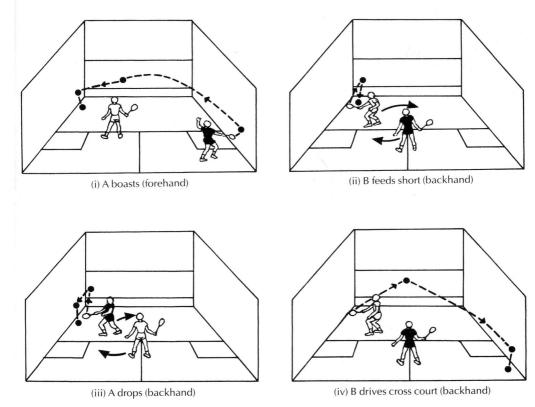

(i) A boasts (forehand)

(ii) B feeds short (backhand)

(iii) A drops (backhand)

(iv) B drives cross court (backhand)

Drill 91 (i)–(iv)

Practice Games

(93) Players may only win a rally with a drop.

(94) After the serve, the game is played entirely in front of the short line.

(95) One or both players must always play a drop after a boast and lose the rally if they do not attempt to do so.

(96) Players score a bonus point if they win the rally with a drop.

LOB

The lob needs to be played slowly and high enough to be out of easy volleying reach of the opponent. The shot should die close to the back corner and is usually played across the court as a recovery shot. Played well it gives a player time to reach a good position before their opponent can hit the ball. Note: targets for the cross-court lob are the same as those shown for the high lob serve.

Coaching Points

(i) The same sideways position used for drives should be used to play the straight lob but turned a bit more towards the front wall for the cross-court lob.

(ii) The contact point is much further forward so that the racket can get under the ball.

(iii) The ball is hit with a very open racket

35

Phil Kenyon makes sure he keeps his eye on the ball for this forehand drop.

face and the follow-through is high, to lift the ball high on the front wall.

Solo Practices

(97) Play a weak high boast and return it with a straight or cross-court lob.
(98) Rally down the side wall, play a short straight shot and return it with a lob.

Pairs Practices

All practices which include a drive played from the front of the court can be used to practise lobs. Some of the most useful ones are:

(i)   drill 11 – Boast and drive (lob);
(ii)   drill 13 – Boast and two drives. The first drive after the boast is played as a lob;
(iii) drill 22 – Boast and cross-court drive (lob);
(iv)   drill 25 – Boast, cross court (lob), straight.

(99) Drop and lob. A feeds a short, straight shot, B lobs straight. The straight lob must not

be played too close to the side wall because the risk of putting it out of court is too great.

Practices for Three

Drill 17 can be used for straight lobs.

Practice Games

(100)   One or both players must always play a lob after a drop or boast; they lose the rally if they do not attempt to do so.

2   Physical Fitness

WHAT IS PHYSICAL FITNESS?

Physical fitness is a subject which is frequently discussed by players, usually in the bar. As fitness and health are hot topics for the media at the moment, an apparent wealth of advice is available for those interested in developing this important aspect of their game. There are, however, one or two important decisions to be taken before you start. Consider two athletes, a shot putter and a middle-distance runner. Both are highly trained, both are fit but they appear totally dissimilar. Each will use very different types of training in their preparation. A major reason for this is demonstrated by Fig 1.

Fitness is a term which is made up of a number of components; being fit for a particular activity means that the balance between these components is correct for that activity. If you try playing a different game, unless the physical demands are similar, you will tire quickly.

Getting the balance right is also important because improvements in one component may result in a decrease in another. Lots of strength work for example, might produce a very strong but inflexible athlete; the stereotype of the muscle-bound weight-lifter.

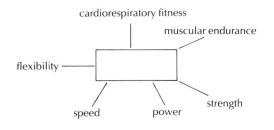

Fig 1   A model of physical fitness for sport.

This is by no means inevitable but care must be taken to balance the training. But there is more; training in one area, power for example, is sometimes best when built on a base of another, in this case strength work. Designing a training programme is a question of the pros and cons – the balance is the essential consideration.

Each individual starts out with better potential in some areas than in others. Part of their success in sport may be dependent on choosing the activity for which they are naturally endowed. This should not prevent anyone from training however, since whatever a person's size or shape, improved fitness (suitable for squash) will always result in an improvement in their ability to play.

Principles of Fitness Training

To design an effective training programme, you must consider certain principles which apply to all the components. You can remember them by using the mnemonic FITTS. They are:

(i)   **F**requency.
(ii)   **I**ntensity.
(iii) **T**ime.
(iv)   **T**ype of exercise.
(v)   **S**pecificity.

The frequency of exercise is the number of sessions you do in a certain time period, usually a week. Many athletes in full-time training will complete three or four sessions a day. Depending on your current level of fitness, however, noticeable improvements will be obtained from three or four sessions a week.

The intensity of an exercise will vary as a percentage of your absolute best effort. This is a useful idea since it relates your workload to your ability. Two people doing a strength exercise like a bench press may be using different weights but both may be working at the same intensity, say 65 per cent of their best single effort.

The time spent in training is the third factor which determines the training load. This simply means how hard you are working. The idea is that you should always work at a level which is just beyond what you have achieved to date. This principle, called progressive overload, is shown in Fig 2.

The training load will vary depending on the combination of frequency, intensity and time expended. If the load is too low the training effect – your improvement in fitness – will be less than it could be. Too great a load is even worse since your system may collapse under the strain. Stress injuries, frequent nagging infections (colds, sprains and so on) and general feelings of tiredness which you cannot shake off are all common signs of overtraining. To avoid this, start slowly and gradually increase the demands of your sessions. More frequent sessions of lower intensity are preferable to an all-out blast once a week.

The type of exercise and the specificity refer to the earlier point about developing the *balance* of fitness necessary for your sport. Hence the squash player is likely to spend more time on aerobic, endurance training rather than shifting heavy weights in the local gym. However, some strength training is important. Getting power in your shots and conditioning your body to withstand the strain of rapid acceleration and changes of direction require a good level of basic strength.

One final point not included in the FITTS model is reversibility. However fit you are, you must continue to train if you are to maintain that level. Virtually all the beneficial

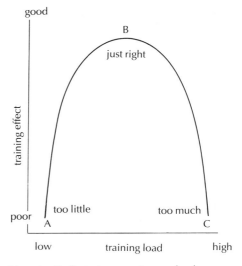

Note: A→B effect of progressive overload

Fig 2   Progressive overload.

effects of training are reversed once you stop – this includes muscle development. The old myth about bulky muscle turning to fat is not true; you just return to how you were before you began training.

COMPONENTS OF FITNESS FOR SQUASH

The sections above should have shown that your training must be based on an assessment of the physical demands of squash. A rough guide to the balance of the various components is shown in Fig 3. The rest of this chapter aims to examine each of the components in detail and provide you with suitable exercises and regimes. But first, a word about an important consideration for any sport, the warm-up.

The Warm-up

Squash is a very fast, physically demanding game which can place a great deal of stress

Fitness components	Not very important	Useful	Important	Very important
Cardiorespiratory fitness				★
Muscular endurance			★	
Strength		★		
Power			★	
Speed (and agility)				★
Flexibility			★	

Fig 3   Fitness components for squash.

on your body. A good warm-up is an essential part of your preparation for play or training if you are to avoid injury and produce your best performance. The warm-up consists of two parts: a general section and a sport-specific section.

In the general warm-up, total body movements like jogging or callisthenics are used to raise the pulse rate and get you sweating. This is followed by a series of soft stretching exercises to loosen the muscles. In this context, soft stretching means that you work to the limit of your flexibility but not beyond it. Hard stretching, which aims to increase the limits, is described on pages 57–62. Both types use similar exercises, however, and you will see suitable stretches for your warm-up described on pages 60–61.

The sport-specific section of the warm-up prepares your body for the exact movements that you will use in the game. On court, shuttles, 'knocking up' and full-power strokes are examples of the types of movement used. These movements also provide a useful warm-up for the brain as well! (See Chapter 5 on Mental Training for more details.)

On completion of the match or the training session, it is not advisable just to stop dead. A cool-down, which follows the same procedure as the general warm-up, helps to prevent muscle stiffness which may well contribute to later injury. Always stretch off and relax for a while before you shower.

Cardiorespiratory Fitness

Cardiorespiratory fitness (CRF), or stamina as it is sometimes called, is one of the bases on which high levels of fitness are built. Virtually all sports require a reasonable level of CRF, if only so that athletes can recover quickly from bouts of exercise. CRF is also a major consideration for health-based fitness, which might be one of your main reasons for playing the game. CRF is developed by aerobic exercise which uses the first major energy system. Aerobic means that the heart and lungs can provide sufficient oxygen to meet the demands of the exercise. Thus oxygen is being shifted from the atmosphere to the muscles at a rate which meets the body's requirements. If the demands exceed the supply rate, the individual starts to work anaerobically; in this context, anaerobic means without oxygen. Obviously some oxygen is still getting through but an insufficient supply results in a different energy-producing chemical reaction in the muscles. Once you begin to work anaerobically, waste products like lactic acid start to accumulate in your body and you will find it difficult to carry on at the same performance level. This represents the second type of energy system available. There is a third energy system in the body which is used for really short bursts of high-intensity work. These three systems are compared in Fig 4.

Aerobic training mostly involves steady rhythmic activities like running, swimming, cycling and dance. As a result of sustained exercise the body becomes more efficient at shifting oxygen to, and removing waste from, the muscles. This, in turn, raises the work intensity at which you begin to work anaerobically. If this level is quite high, the athlete can meet most of the demands of the sport from the aerobic system and avoid the negative effects on performance that inevitably result if anaerobic work is performed for too long. If you notice the state of a 400m runner at the end of a race, the complete exhaustion is a result of high intensity, predominantly anaerobic work. However, his high aerobic fitness base means that he recovers quickly. Anaerobic training will be examined in detail on pages 42–44.

You can see that aerobic training must be sub-maximal – below your absolute limit. One big problem is deciding on a suitable intensity. A crude method is to try talking to your partner as you work. If you can just about have a conversation but maintain the work rate, your speed is about right. A better and more accurate measure can be obtained from your heartbeat. To be optimally effective, your aerobic work rate should exceed a certain limit – the training threshold. This can be calculated as a percentage of your maximum pulse. Take 220 minus your age – this represents your maximum heart rate. The training zone falls between 60 and 90 per cent of this number.

For example:

Person: Mr R. Acket
Age: 30 years
Maximum heart rate: 220–30 = 190
Training threshold: 190 × 0.6 = 144 beats
                     per minute (bpm)
Upper limit: 190 × 0.9 = 171 bpm

Therefore Mr Acket trains at a speed which results in a fairly constant pulse of between 144 and 171 bpm. When you get reasonably fit, experience has shown that this level is a little low. You can use the simpler method of adding 25 to your age and subtracting this from 220.

For example:

Person: Ms I. Yellowspot
Age: 28 years
Target heart rate: 220–53 = 157 bpm

When you are at rest, take your pulse at the neck or the wrist by resting two fingers over the spot and counting for fifteen seconds.

ENERGY SYSTEMS			
	1	**2**	**3**
Duration	0–15 secs	15secs–2mins	Over 2mins
Technical term	ATP–PC system	LA (lactic acid)	Aerobic system
Description	Strength, power, speed	Short-term muscular endurance	Long-term muscular endurance and aerobic activity
Squash activities	Hard Serve	Rallies	Recovery between games

Fig 4   *The main energy systems of the body and their practical meaning in squash.*

FITTS Component	Minimum criteria
Frequency	3 times per week
Intensity	Elevated heart rate between 60–90% of maximum, or 220 – (age +25) beats per minute
Time	20 minutes
Type (of exercise)	Gross body exercise, such as running, swimming, cycling.
Specificity	Long duration, low-intensity shuttle running.

Fig 5   The FITTS principle as applied to cardiorespiratory fitness training.

Multiply by four (or double and double) to obtain your heart rate. Do not press too hard. Once you are working you should be able to feel your heartbeat by placing a hand over your heart. With practice you will be able to take your pulse as you exercise, which is always more reliable than taking it once you have finished. An excellent alternative is to use one of the basic heart rate monitors currently available commercially. Use your working heart rate to monitor the intensity of your training sessions.

The FITTS principle which has been outlined is applied to aerobic training in Fig 5. This shows the level of work necessary to achieve real improvements in this fitness component.

Due to the specificity principle, running would seem to be the most effective exercise for squash, although other methods like swimming could and should be used. For this purpose, a proper pair of running shoes would be a sound investment so as to avoid injury; running on soft ground will also help. If the prospect of cross-country running does not appeal to you, the use of training drills, as long as they meet the criteria set for aerobic training is just as good. (*See* Chapter 1.) Indeed, this is a sensible factor to include in your programme to check if your skills can stand up to the pressures of fatigue – an inevitable part of competition. Take care that

the skill drills you use are simple though, since when you are tired errors will creep in. Aerobic training is important but not if it ruins your technique.

Anaerobic training is also an important consideration for squash players since many long rallies will be physically intense. Your body must be able to cope with the demands of working anaerobically and be able to recover quickly before the next rally. The most usual way to develop anaerobic fitness is by some form of interval training. The idea behind interval training is that the short rest between bursts of quite intense workloads only permits a partial recovery. The two main varieties of interval training are shown in Fig 6.

Interval training is more specific to squash because it matches more closely the actual demands of a game situation. The important decisions here relate to the type and intensity of work compared to the length of rest interval. As a general rule, longer work periods of lower intensity and shorter rests result in a more aerobic session. Comparatively shorter work periods of higher intensity together with a longer rest produce a greater anaerobic effect. This would be called a higher quality session and would be used during the season and/or closer to the event for which you are preparing. Fig 7 contrasts four sample sessions, two of each kind.

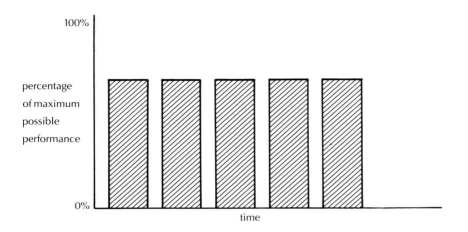

Aerobic intervals – lower intensity, longer work periods, shorter rests

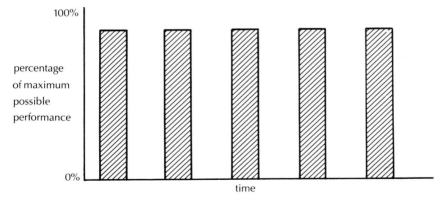

Anaerobic intervals – higher intensity, shorter work periods, longer rests

Fig 6   The interval training principle.

AEROBIC	
General	Specific
6 × 600m at three-quarter pace, with 15 seconds recovery	Touch each corner of the court returning to the T between corners. Rest 10 seconds. Repeat the cycle twelve times.

ANAEROBIC	
General	Specific
6 × 60m sprints 2 minutes recovery	Number each corner of the court. Your partner calls out a sequence e.g. 1–3–4–2. You touch the corners in that sequence, then in reverse order, returning to the T between corners. Rest for 90 seconds. Repeat the cycle five times.

Fig 7   Interval training sessions for squash.

As mentioned above, anaerobic work is built on the base of aerobic fitness. High-quality interval training is dependent on your ability to recover quickly. Lack of aerobic-base fitness will result in only partial recovery and as a result lower quality (i.e. below maximum) performance on the work periods.

As you will see later, monitoring your progress is an important element of fitness training. Keeping a note of your performance will also enable you to ensure proper progressive overload. Aerobic fitness can be monitored quite easily. Record your time over a set course, say three miles, and repeat the run at regular intervals. Your time may vary slightly because of other variables, weather, motivation, etc., but in general, improvements in performance will provide an indicator of your current fitness level. Assessing your anaerobic condition is slightly harder but by considering two factors you should reach a reasonable conclusion.

Notice the drop off in performance which occurs as you do the repetitions. Unless you deliberately take it easy on the first repetition, a more consistent performance will be indicative of greater anaerobic condition. Monitoring your recovery is another useful technique. See how low your pulse rate falls in the rest interval. Alternatively, relate your rest interval directly to your pulse. In a 6 × 200m session for example, you could start the next run once your heart rate has dropped to 140bpm. Record your time for the whole session and use this as your measure. These are only rough indicators though; proper assessment requires sophisticated electronic monitoring equipment but these techniques will give you a reasonable idea.

Strength, Endurance and Power

The whole of this section is concerned with different aspects of muscle fitness. With all the information available and the many and varied myths about building muscles, this can be a very confusing area. To avoid this, the first step is to define the various terms which are commonly used. These are shown in Fig 8.

As with the components of fitness, each of

Term	Definition
Strength	The maximum force that a muscle, or group of muscles, can generate. Sometimes the statement 'at a specified speed or velocity' can be added to this definition because force will diminish as the speed of the limb increases.
Muscular endurance	The ability of the muscle or muscle group to continue applying force.
Power	The product of force and velocity; in simpler terms strength × speed.
Flexibility	Range of motion about a joint or series of joints.

Fig 8   Definition of terms applied to muscle fitness.

(i)

Fig 9   Muscular endurance exercises.
　　(i)　　Press ups.
　　(ii)　　Pull-ups.
　　(iii)　Sit-ups.
　　(iv)　Back extensions.

(ii)

these different factors is related and in some way dependent on the others. Once again, what is necessary is the correct balance of factors for your sport and your particular strengths and weaknesses.

Improvements in muscle fitness are obtained by getting a muscle or group of muscles to work in isolation against a resistance which is greater than normal. This does not necessarily require a great deal of equipment. Fig 9 shows some body-weight exercises which are commonly used for muscular endurance training. Most use a change in body position to place a group of muscles under stress. The press-up, for example, works on the muscles of the chest and upper arm.

In these examples the extra resistance is relatively low and your body will quickly adapt to the loads involved. The overload

(iii)

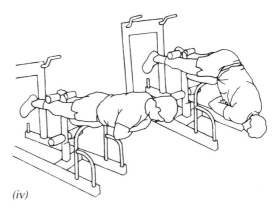

(iv)

45

principle will therefore mean a very large number of repetitions if you are to gain any benefit. For this reason, most muscle training involves the use of weights or machines like a multi-gym to provide additional resistance. Indeed, as you will see in Fig 10, improving strength will require comparatively high resistances which cannot easily be obtained with the body-weight callisthenics described previously.

Weight-training, as with so many other sport-related topics, is rife with misinformation, myths and even absolute nonsense. To sort out right from wrong requires a knowledge of the fundamental principles and a questioning approach to the advice offered. With all advice, including this chapter, look for an explanation of the reasons behind the advice; ask the expert to justify his wisdom by relating it to physiological principles and actual examples. This approach should dismiss some of the widely held beliefs about strength. For example: Weight-training makes you slow – sprinters use weights, are they slow? Weight-training makes women more masculine – can you think of feminine and attractive female athletes? The chances are they all use weight-training as part of their preparation.

For squash the most useful types of muscle fitness are muscular endurance (LME) and power. Massive strength is not really necessary although, as you will see, power work is built on a base of strength development. Consideration of how your muscles work may help to clarify the reasons for the different types of exercise used. This is shown (in fairly simple terms) in Figs 11 and 12.

As you can see, the different types of muscle fibre are used for different jobs and are recruited (used) in a set order depending on the intensity and duration of the exercise. Low intensity, long-term exercise uses slow twitch (ST) type I fibres. Fast twitch (FT) type II fibres will be called in first for high intensity, short duration work. Type IIb fibres are really fast but have very poor endurance compared to IIa fibres which come into action if high intensity work continues for longer than about two seconds. As a con-

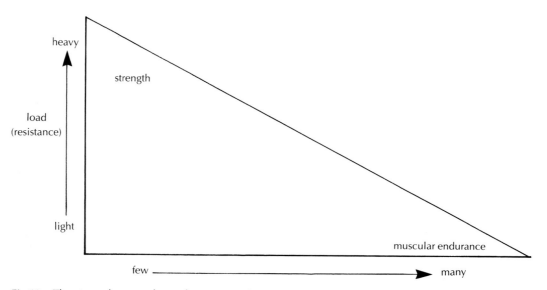

Fig 10   The strength-muscular endurance continuum.

Characteristics	Slow twitch	Fast twitch
Aerobic capacity	High	Low
Anaerobic capacity	Low	High
Contraction time	Slow	Fast
Force	Low	High
Activities	Endurance-type	Sprint/explosive-type
Fatigue	Slow	Fast

Fig 11   Summary of characteristics of fast- and slow-twitch muscle fibres, adapted from Fox, E.L., Sports Physiology *(Saunders College, 1979).*

sequence, training for fast, high power movements is most effective when high loads (weights) are used for few repetitions, probably six or less. In certain circumstances FT fibres are also recruited for low load work which involves very fast movements; a squash shot is an excellent example (*see* Fleck and Kraemer, 1987). All this theory has important implications for strength and power training which will become obvious in the next section.

Developing Strength and Power

Training in this area means you can use a variety of equipment and regimes. This variety can be broken down into four main categories:

(i)   Isometric; from the Greek, *iso* meaning same and *metric* meaning measure or, in this context, length. In this mode the muscle is very tense but the limbs do not move. Big strength gains are possible using this mode. Static contractions, tightening the muscles but not moving and the Bullworker, are examples of the isometric mode. Static work is very useful for rehabilitation but the specificity principle means that exercises in which you do not move are not very useful for squash. Only the grip on the racket requires static strength. Isometric contrac-

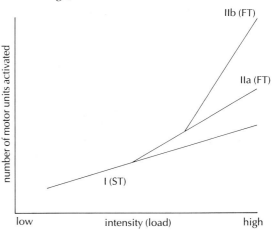

Fig 12   Recruitment pattern of muscle fibres.

tions result in large blood pressure increases. For this reason, isometric work should not be used by old people or those with circulatory problems.

(ii)   Isokinetic; the 'same speed' mode, uses a mechanical device to limit the speed of movement. If the athlete tries to move more quickly, the load on his muscles effectively increases. As a result, provided the athlete tries hard, the muscle is always loaded to the maximum possible. This mode is very useful for swimming, small muscle movements and skills which would be changed if extra weight resistance was used. Squash serves would benefit from this training but genuine

National Champion Del Harris looking to cut the ball off on the volley.

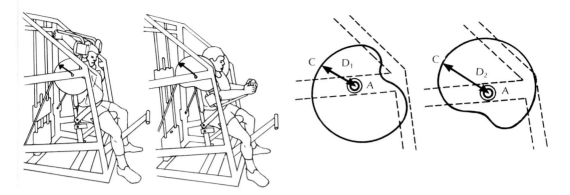

Fig 13   The dynamic variable resistance principle on a Nautilus machine.

isokinetic machines are rare and usually expensive.

(iii)   Isotonic; 'same tension' training is by far the most common type of weights exercise. A fixed weight, a barbell, dumb-bell or machine lever is moved by the muscles. In fact, because the muscle is strongest in the middle range of its movement (half-way between the most extended and the most contracted position), the muscle's tension– how hard it is working – changes throughout the movement. Isotonic training can use free weights, discs attached to a long bar held with both hands (a barbell) or a short bar held in one hand (a dumb-bell). Alternatively, machines like multi-gyms may be used. The relative merits of each will be examined on page 50.

(iv)   Dynamic Variable Resistance (DVR); this new 'sub mode' represents an attempt to combine the advantages of isotonic and isokinetic training. DVR machines attempt to vary the load on the muscle to match its effective strength. Such machines use levers or cams to increase the load on the muscle through the movement. An example is given in Fig 13 which shows a Nautilus machine. The weight load is determined, in part, by the distance of the chain attachment (C) from the axle (A) of the eccentric cam. As the lever is lowered, this distance increases and the load becomes greater. This idea seems attractive but the main problem lies in how closely the adjusted load matches the 'strength curve' of the muscles. Variable resistance machines may therefore offer little advantage over the orthodox isotonic equipment.

(v)   Plyometrics; a comparatively recent idea, imported from track and field athletics, plyometrics uses only body-weight but increases the intensity of use by jumping from/to heights or bouncing. This mode is based on the idea that prior to contracting explosively, the muscle stretches slightly to prime itself for the movement. Try for yourself by squatting down slightly and then jumping into the air. Your body will bob down before you jump. As a result the quadriceps, the muscles on the front of the leg, will stretch, then rapidly contract to push you up. Jumping with no downward movement will result in a less explosive contraction and you will not reach as high in the air. Plyometrics are excellent for developing such explosive movements and are ideal for squash which requires such rapid acceleration and changes in direction. It is, however, a very intensive and high-quality mode and is only suitable for limited use by well-conditioned athletes. Injury will rapidly occur if plyometric exercises are attempted too often or without the right level of basic strength.

Within each of these modes, exercises can be designed either as general or sport specific. All muscle training requires a good basic preparation of general strength and power which is usually repeated every season in the same way as an aerobic build-up is used in preparation for later, more specific work. The general exercises provide an all-round development which enables the muscles and joints to withstand and benefit from the sport-specific exercises. These are designed to match more closely the actual movements made in squash.

A variety of different exercises from both categories are shown in Fig 16–30. Make sure that you use the diagrams in conjunction with the information provided in Figs 14, 15, 31 and 32. Note that some exercises are only possible with machines, some with free weights but they all use equipment generally available to you. As a general rule, working with free weights is preferable for a variety of reasons, particularly since such exercise will develop the 'fixator' muscles which help to hold you steady in the required position. This development helps to assure the integrity (stability) of the joints involved. Machines are less effective in doing this since the weight

Figure	Exercise	Major muscles involved	Equipment
16	Power clean	Hips, legs, back (power development)	Barbell
17	Front squat	Hips, legs (quadriceps)	Barbell
18	Leg extension	Quadriceps	Machine
19	Leg Curls	Hamstrings	Machine
20	Bench press	Chest, triceps, shoulders	Barbell or machine
21	V-sits	Abdominals	No equipment
22	Pull downs	Latissimus dorsi (side of back)	Machine or pulley

Fig 14   General resistance exercises for squash.

Figure	Exercise	Major muscles involved	Equipment
23	Split squats	Quadriceps and hips	Barbell
24	Dumb-bell flys	Chest	Dumb-bells
25	Single-arm cheat rowing	Trunk rotators and upper back	Dumb-bell
26	Wrist Circles	Forearms	Dumb-bell
27	Dead lift	Lower back	Barbell
28	Bent over rowing	Upper and lower back	Barbell
29	Twisting V-sits	Abdominals and oblique abdominals	None
30	Plyometric depth jumps	Legs	Benches/gym boxes and mats

Fig 15   Specific resistance exercises for squash.

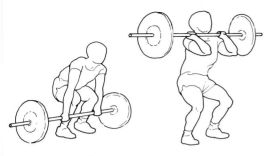

Fig 16   Power clean.

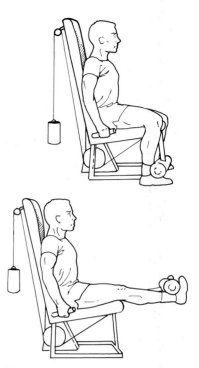

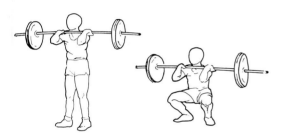

Fig 17   Front squat.

Fig 18   Leg extension.

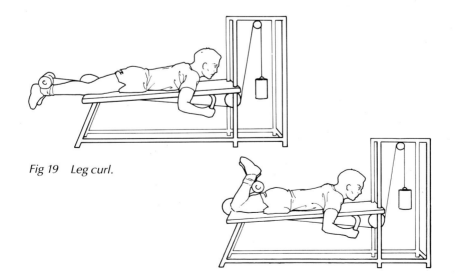

Fig 19   Leg curl.

Fig 21   V-sits.

Fig 20   Bench press.

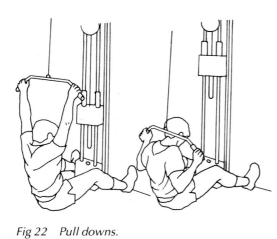

Fig 23   Split squats.

Fig 22   Pull downs.

Fig 24   Dumb-bell flys.

Fig 25   Single-arm dumb-bell pulls.

Fig 26   Wrist circles with dumb-bells.

Fig 27   Dead lift.

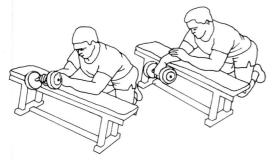

Fig 28   Bent over rowing.

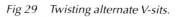

Fig 29   Twisting alternate V-sits.

Fig 30   Plyometric depth jumps.

Figure	Exercise	Starting position	Movement	Other points
16	Power clean	Feet under bar, hip-width apart. Shoulder-width overgrasp grip. Hips below shoulders. Arms straight, back flat.	Lift bar from floor with straight arms and keep back flat. Extend body. Keep bar close in. Turn wrists over and receive bar on front of shoulders. Bend legs to receive bar. Lower to thighs, then to floor.	Have bar 20 cm off the floor to start with. Use blocks or wooden disks for this. Make movement smooth and, later, fast and dynamic.
17	Front squat	Bar on chest, high elbows. Feet flat just outside hip-width.	Squat under control to 'thighs parallel'. Return to standing. Keep chest up throughout.	Avoid deep ballistic squatting.
18	Leg extension	Feet under lower pads. Sit upright.	Extend legs; lower under control.	
19	Leg curl	Face down on machine, heels under top pads.	Bring heels up towards buttocks. Return under control.	
20	Bench press	Lie face up on a bench. Hips, shoulders, head all on bench. Shoulder-width grip of bar.	Lower bar to chest. Extend arms until fully straightened.	If using a barbell rather than machine, beginners may find it easier to balance if they start the exercise with the bar on the chest.
21	V-sits	Lie on back	Lift body and bend knees until knees and chest meet. Return to start position.	
22	Latissimus pull-down	Seated or kneeling. Wide overgrasp grip of bar, arms fully extended.	Pull bar down to base of the neck. Return under control.	

Fig 31   Explanation of general weight-training exercises.

lever is obviously fixed by the machine against all except the main movement.

Planning your Muscle Training

Developing a weight-training programme is a skilled business. Fleck and Kraemer, whose book is recommended in the Further Reading section, highlight the 'needs assessment' which is necessary for really effective programme design. Discussion between a squash authority (yourself or a coach) and suitably qualified strength trainers is

required. The British Amateur Weight Lifters' Association (BAWLA) provides such training and also offers consultancy on sessions for members. The contact address is provided in the list at the back of the book. Some suggested sessions to get you started are provided in Figs 33 and 34.

Each session will consist of a warm-up, exercises arranged to work different body parts and a cool-down. The FITTS principle is used to vary the sessions depending on the phase of training. A more complete consideration of this phasing, termed periodisation, is

Figure	Exercise	Starting position	Movement	Other points
23	Split squat	Bar on front of shoulders, elbows high. Feet split front to back. Front foot flat, rear foot on toes pointing forwards.	Bend front leg and push hips down and forwards. Keep the trunk upright. Push back off the front leg once the thigh is parallel with the floor.	Repeat the exercise with the other foot forwards.
24	Dumb-bell flys	Dumb-bells held above the chest. Arms are straight or held slightly bent. Feet flat on the floor.	Lower the dumb-bells symmetrically to the side until the limit of comfortable movement is reached. Keep the elbows locked – do not bend and straighten as the dumb-bells are lowered and raised.	Lower under control.
25	Single arm cheat rowing	Bend forward and support one arm on an incline bench. With the other arm, hold a dumb-bell. Feet split front to back.	Lift the dumb-bell and rotate the trunk so that the chest faces away from the bench.	Keep the head up and the back flat throughout.
26	Wrist circles	Grasp a dumb-bell and support the forearm on a bench. The dumb-bell may be held vertically or horizontally.	Move the dumb-bell slowly in as wide a circle as possible. The forearms do not move.	Vary the forearm position between palms vertical and palms horizontal.
27	Dead lift	Bar held in the hands resting on the thighs. Head up, back flat.	Bend forwards under control to a comfortable lower limit then straighten. Do not let the bar touch the ground.	Look up and keep the back flat throughout.
28	Bent over rowing	As for dead lift then bend forwards to a maximum angle of 45 degrees. Let the bar hang vertically below the shoulders.	Raise the bar to the chest then lower. Do not try to hold the bar in the top position.	Stand upright before placing the bar on the ground.
29	Twisting V-sits	On the back, hands by the ears or folded across the chest.	Lift and twist the body and the opposite leg so that the right elbow touches the left knee. Lower then repeat on the other side.	Try to avoid jerky movements. Emphasise the twist as you progress.
30	Plyometric depth jumps	Standing on a box or platform.	Jump down onto the floor then immediately spring on to the next box.	Warm up thoroughly. Wear shoes and use mats between the boxes.

Fig 32   Explanation of specific weight-training exercises.

Exercise	Sets/Repetitions	Weight
Power cleans	3 × 10	
Front squat	3 × 10	
Bench press	3 × 10	
Leg extension	3 × 10	
Leg curls	3 × 10	
Pull downs	3 × 10	
V-sits	3 × 20	

Fig 33   An example schedule for pre-competition training.

Exercise	Sets/Repetitions	Weight
Split squats	3 × 10 each leg	
Dumb-bell flys	3 × 10	
Single rowing	3 × 10 each arm	
Dead lift	3 × 10	
Wrist circles	8 circles each way	
Bent rowing	3 × 10	
Twisting V-sits	3 × 24	

Fig 34   An example schedule for competition training.

given in Chapter 6 on Programme Planning.

A final point which is crucial to effective muscle training is the area of safety. As with any training system, weights are effective by placing the body under stress to which it then adjusts. There is a risk of injury which is minimised by attention to safe working practices. Some general guide-lines are as follows:

(i)   Always warm up to sweating before training. Always cool down afterwards.

(ii)   Wear warm and comfortable clothing. Always wear shoes. Remove jewellery before training.

(iii)   Do not train alone. Learn how to 'spot' for others.

(iv)   Use good technique. Poor technique results in injury and a less effective work out.

(v)   Train progressively. Do not push yourself too hard or try to show off.

(vi)   Keep the training environment clean and tidy. Loose weights or a crowded space can cause accidents.

(vii)   When using free weights, frequently

check the collars which hold the weights on to the bar.

Note: heavy weight-training is not recommended for children. In any case, proper trained supervision is essential.

Speed and Agility

A good preparation of strength and power training will give a player the physical agility to move quickly. Speed can also be developed by short sprint drills over ten or twenty metres, a high-quality exercise which may be usefully employed in mid-season training sessions. Quick movement in squash, however, is dependent on a number of factors including agility – the ability to move the body in a smooth and co-ordinated fashion – which is an important consideration. This ability is, in part, a natural attribute which some individuals possess more than others. Fig 35 shows a test of agility, originally designed for American football players, which provides a useful drill. Squash-specific on-court drills can also be designed and their use has already been mentioned.

Speed on court is also a function of the player's reaction time which depends, in turn, on their ability to read the game and pay attention to the correct cues provided by their opponent. Such decision-making drills should also play a part in the player's preparation.

Flexibility

As a component of fitness, flexibility is probably the most neglected area in the vast majority of sports. Only gymnasts, dancers and recently some track athletes seem to spend time on flexibility work. This is unfortunate because increased flexibility, provided that strength levels are maintained, will help to prevent injury and may well enhance your speed. The rider on strength is

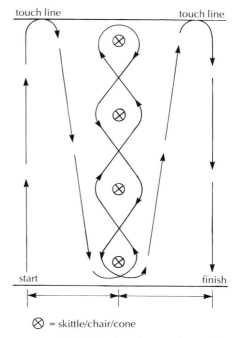

⊗ = skittle/chair/cone

Note: start position is lying face down on floor with hands by the shoulders and head on the start line.

Fig 35   Illinois agility run, reproduced with permission from Adams, J. et al., Foundations of Physical Activity (Stipes, 1965).

important since very mobile joints may be even more liable to damage than stiff ones. This is particularly noticeable after injury when weakened muscles and loosened ligaments mean more flexibility but extreme danger of further damage.

This apart, improved flexibility is a worthwhile aim for performers in any sport and is also an important consideration in health-related fitness. As mentioned earlier, stretching exercises may be soft (not to the limit but performed as an important component of the warm-up) or hard (designed to improve your mobility). Three techniques may be used:

(i)   Static stretching is the most common and simplistic method to use. The muscle is

Figure	Exercise	Muscles stretched	Starting position	Movement	Other points
38	Calf stretch	Calf	Lean against wall, foot pointing forwards	(i) To stretch outer calf, keep leg straight and push heel into ground. Push hips forwards. (ii) To stretch inner calf (soleus), bend leg and push forwards and downwards with hip. Keep heel on ground.	Vary position of toes.
39	Hamstring and lower back stretch	Hamstrings, lower back	Sit on floor, feet together and legs straight.	Sit up first (chest out) then stretch forwards to the toes.	Vary leg positions (apart).
40	Hip stretch	Front of hip	Lunge position on floor.	Push hips forwards.	Progress to more upright trunk position with rear foot on toes.
41	Groin stretch	Groin, inside thighs	Sit on floor, legs folded with soles of feet together.	Gently ease knees outwards and downwards.	Use pressure from arms if necessary.
42	Side stretch	Side (oblique) abdominals	Upright stance, feet astride.	Bend sideways and hold position.	Avoid leaning forwards.
43	Shoulder stretch	Shoulders, chest	(i) Standing. (ii) Seated – leg in front.	Lift arms upwards and backwards. Partner lifts arms upwards and backwards, or sideways.	(iii) If partner places a knee in the back of the exerciser, this can help stability.
44	Wrist stretch	Forearms	Kneeling on floor, hands flat.	Fingers pointing towards the body, pull shoulders back to stretch forearms.	Change direction of fingers.
45	Arm stretch	Shoulder, side of chest	Kneeling on all fours, arm out-stretched.	Pull shoulder back to produce stretch on top of shoulder, arm and side of chest.	Reach out with hand first.
46	Abdominal stretch	Stomach	Lie face-up on floor.	Extend stomach upwards as much as possible.	Support body on feet and shoulders.

Fig 36   Explanations of static flexibility exercises.

gradually stretched to a state of mild tension. This position is held for at least ten seconds, then the muscle is slowly relaxed. With time, your movement limit increases.

(ii) Dynamic or ballistic stretching is a more risky business. The muscle is stretched as before but, once the limit is reached, small bouncing movements are used to exceed it gradually. Research has criticised ballistic stretching as a cause of injury but some competitive athletes find it more effective in improving flexibility. You must decide for yourself if rapid gains are worth the risk. You should at least take precautions to minimise the injury risks by completing a comprehensive warm-up, including static stretching, before you start the ballistic work.

(iii) Proprioceptive neuromuscular facilita- tion (PNF) is another import from athletics which has revolutionised training methods in other sports. In PNF work the muscle is held by a partner at your limit of movement. The muscle under tension (the one to be stretched) is then contracted against your partner's resistance for about ten seconds. As this muscle is relaxed, partner pressure or contracting the opposite, antagonistic muscle will result in an increase in flexibility. Most exercises can be adapted to the PNF mode provided that some apparatus or a partner can be used to provide resistance and stretching force. Take care that the stretching force applied is not excessive or the muscle will either be injured or automatically tighten, hence defeating the aim of the whole procedure.

Figure	Exercise	Muscles stretched	Starting position	Movement	Other points
52	PNF Hamstring stretch	Hamstrings	Sitting on floor, feet together and legs straight.	Contraction: push back against partner and push down into the ground with both legs (10secs), then relax. Stretch: reach forwards (with or without partner assistance) towards toes.	
53	PNF shoulder stretch	Shoulder, chest	Sitting or kneeling, arms outstretched to the side, parallel with floor.	Contraction: pull arms forwards against partner resistance (10secs), then relax. Stretch: partner pulls arms back, keeping them parallel to the floor.	Can also be done with arms above head.

Fig 37 Explanations of PNF flexibility exercises.

Fig 38   Calf stretch.

Fig 39   Hamstring and lower back stretch.

Fig 40   Hip stretch.

Fig 41   Groin stretch.

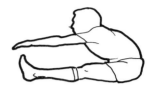

Fig 42   Side stretch.

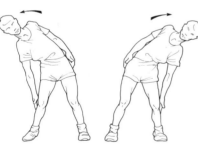

Fig 43   Shoulder stretch.

Fig 44   Wrist stretch.

Fig 45   Arm stretch.

Fig 46   Abdominal stretch.

Fig 47   PNF hamstring stretch.

Fig 48   PNF shoulder stretch.

Fig 49   Ballistic standing toe touch.

Fig 50   Hurdler stretch.

FITTS Component	Suggested Guide-lines
Frequency	Can be done every day once experience has been gained. Initially, every other day.
Intensity	To the point of tension in the muscle i.e. the no pain (but slight ache!) limit.
Time	Hold each exercise for ten to twenty seconds. Each session will take about thirty minutes including warm-up.
Type (of exercise)	In the early stages, use only static stretches. As you progress, include PNF work to develop your flexibility.
Specificity	Pay particular attention to those leg muscles involved in forward/backward and side-to-side movements. Always include general flexibility work since squash can involve a wide variety of movements.

Fig 51   FITTS principle as applied to flexibility exercises.

Exercises for flexibility are illustrated in Figs 38–50 and instructions for their use are provided in Figs 36, 37 and 51.

Some exercises are contra-indicated unless such flexibility is specifically required. Hurdler's splits, for example, place a great strain on the knee and unless you are a hurdler, there are better options available to you.

3   Healthy Eating

Competitors must be well prepared physically on the day of competition. This preparation involves many training sessions over the previous months or years. Food has been providing the energy for body maintenance and general day-to-day activity as well as providing the energy needed to train. Nutrients in the food – protein, vitamins and minerals – have been used to replenish body losses incurred each day. Food is crucial for our health and well-being as well as allowing us to play squash.

Food can also be important to us on psychological and social levels. It may be psychologically important to eat favourite foods before a game as they are believed to help performance. These foods (often highly peculiar to an individual) may indeed ensure that peak performance is reached but it is unlikely to be because our bodies need the nutrients physiologically. However, if eating a certain food helps us to have that winning confidence then that is what matters. Sometimes, as we shall see later, there are certain foods which should be avoided on physiological grounds as they can damage performance.

On a social level food gives us great pleasure; we all enjoy eating with a group of friends. Often the group will decide where or what to eat. Serious athletes may find themselves somewhere where the choice is limited and perhaps not quite suitable. Players may therefore have to choose foods which they know are unsuitable. If this happens on an occasional basis it does not matter, but if it is a regular occurrence it is important to ask why this is the case and whether performance is affected. It therefore correlates with the question of whether performance can be improved by eating foods which are more likely to be beneficial to performance.

Eating for your sport can be broken down into two subdivisions: eating for training (as this happens regularly and repeatedly, food choice must satisfy demands of training as well as good, general health) and eating for competition. Both are influenced by who we are, where we are and the company we keep.

REQUIREMENTS FOR FOOD

Eating and drinking are taken for granted by most people. We eat and drink without too much thought and assume that our bodily needs will be met and, indeed, most of the time they will. But whether these needs are being met optimally is the question that all serious sports people and their coaches should address.

The human body is marvellously resilient, tolerant and versatile. If food-energy intake is less than the body needs the body simply conserves energy in order to 'balance the books'. People on reducing diets have been observed to be less active and physically slower (thereby conserving energy) than before embarking on their diet. This has implications for the athlete who is training and at the same time deliberately reducing food intake. Is the same effort being put into the training or, indeed, can it be? Young children when fed less than they need become less active and grow less quickly as the body attempts to balance its 'energy books'. If a young player is exercising hard and not able to eat a sufficient amount, it is likely that growth and/or the level of effort sustainable will suffer. It is not possible to obtain energy if insufficient energy foods are consumed.

However, there comes a point when the body can no longer adapt to an insufficient intake of food-energy and at this point general body functions begin to deteriorate very noticeably. Body tissues are not repaired efficiently (injury may take longer to heal) or there is weight loss; levels of activity become poor and general health often deteriorates with increased likelihood of infection. Professional medical investigation and treatment may be essential at this point.

The body thus has an adaptive capability and a deficiency response. At the other end of the spectrum (and much more likely to occur in Western countries), the body reacts to excessive food-energy intake. Food consumption above requirement will not raise the level of activity or turn individuals into super-performers, although it will encourage rapid growth – in children upwards, and in adults outwards. Eating more protein than the body needs or can use, simply results in the excess being excreted. The same is true of water-soluble vitamins such as vitamin C and some minerals such as sodium chloride (salt). In the case of fat-soluble vitamins such as vitamin A and certain minerals such as iron which the body cannot so easily dispose of, excess stores can ultimately be life-threatening. Players, therefore, need to take special care with regard to the dangers of over-indulgence, especially when it comes to diet supplements. Regular monitoring of body-weight can provide information about meeting nutrient requirements or meeting them in excess.

Indeed, there is a publication entitled *Recommended Amounts of Food Energy and Nutrients for Groups of People in the UK* (DHSS, 1979) which provides a useful guide. There is no evidence that sports people need any more nutrients than non-sports people, providing that they are eating a good variety of foods which will meet their energy needs. These needs may well vary from season to season and during different training periods. The total amount of food, as well as the type of food which is consumed, may also vary.

In summary, the overall needs of the player in training will be both unique and, in that individual, variable. This variation may be masked by the ability of the individual to adapt to different levels of nutrition, but it is essential that such adaptation is not allowed to mask impending deficiency. Players and their coaches must remain vigilant.

WHAT IS IN FOOD?

Food is a mixture of nutrients: fat, carbohydrates, protein, vitamins and minerals. Everyone needs these nutrients in the same way. Eating food ultimately enables these nutrients to be made available to our bodies. All naturally occurring foods contain all nutrients, but in differing amounts (dependent upon the function which the food performed in the plant or the animal). For example, leaves are not storage organs and so their energy content is low. Meat, however, is largely muscle so it has a high protein content.

In Figs 52 and 53 there is a list of foods and some of the nutrients they contain. The carbohydrate and fat foods provide the most energy in our diets but you will see that they also can provide protein, vitamins and minerals. The lists are put together in a way which allows you to choose amounts of food which provide similar amounts of carbohydrate (CHO), fat and protein. A more comprehensive list is given in the *Manual of Nutrition* (HMSO, 1985).

As foods are mixtures of nutrients it is difficult to say one food is better than another. For example, if we said that cheese was bad because of its fat content and omitted it from our diet then we would also

Sources of Protein

Meat and fish – also rich sources of minerals.
60–85g cooked (not fried) meat* or oily fish
60g hard cheese
85g edam, gouda, brie or similar cheese
3 grilled sausages (add one portion of fat)
For reduced energy and fat:
60–85g cooked chicken (no skin), veal or
   rabbit
60–85g cooked liver*
60–85g white fish
60–85g tuna in brine or 4 pilchards
170g cottage cheese

Each portion supplies about 20–25g protein,
15–20g fat, 200–250kcals.

Each portion supplies about 20–25g protein,
5g fat, 150kcals, but do not fry or add fat

Sources of Carbohydrate

(Milk and milk products also provide significant amounts of calcium).
1 glass of milk   Supplies about 8g protein, 12g CHO, 8g fat, 150kcals.

For reduced energy and fat:
1 glass skimmed milk or 1 carton plain
   yoghurt
Supplies about 8g protein, 12g CHO, 80kcal.

Cereals and legumes – high carbohydrate and some protein.
1 thin/medium slice white bread*
1/2 roll, bun, crumpet, teacake etc.
1 tbs white flour*
1 digestive biscuit
   (also contains one portion of fat)
4 tbs unsweetened breakfast cereal*
3 tbs baked beans* or other cooked bean*/
   pea*/lentil*
   (also contains one third of portion of 'meat'
   protein)
3–4 tbs fresh/processed peas
1 tbs apple crumble/pie
   (also contains one portion of fat and one
   'fruit' carbohydrate portion)

Each portion supplies about 2g protein,
15g CHO as starch and 70kcals.

Fruit and vegetables – also supply important vitamins.
Small apple, pear, orange
1/2 small banana
10–12 cherries or grapes
2 medium plums, prunes, apricots,
   dates (dried)
1 tbs raisins, currants
2 tbs any vegetable (except avocado – add
   four portions of fat)
1 small/medium potato, boiled or baked
   (if fried add one portion of fat)

Each portion supplies about 0–2g protein,
5–10g CHO as sugars and 25–40kcals.

Sources of Fat
Small scrap butter or margarine (5g)
1 tsp oil
2 tsp mayonnaise   Each portion supplies about 5g fat, 45kcals.
1 slice fried streaky bacon
5 olives
10 roasted peanuts
2 tsp double cream
Cereals and legumes   fortified flour products, tofu
Meat and fish   salmon and sardines if bones consumed
Fruit and vegetables   dark-green leafed vegetables
Other   molasses and unhulled sesame seeds (as
                                    in tahini)

Fig 52   Nutrients contained in typical portions of food.

Sources of Thiamin or Vitamin B1
Milk and milk products   all milk and soya milk
Cereals and legumes   all legumes**, fortified (non-wholemeal)
                                    bread**, flour products and fortified breakfast
                                    cereals
Meat and fish   ham and pork products, liver
Fruit and vegetables   none
Other   brewer's yeast

Sources of Riboflavin or Vitamin B2
Milk and milk products   all types of milk**
Cereals and legumes   only fortified breakfast cereals
Meat and fish   liver
Fruit and vegetables   dark-green leafed vegetables
Other   brewer's yeast

Sources of Pyridoxine or Vitamin B6
Milk and milk products   none
Cereals and legumes   all legumes**
Meat and fish   beef, pork, lamb, tuna and salmon
Fruit and vegetables   bananas and potatoes
Other   nuts

Sources of Calcium
Milk and milk products   all milk**, cheese**, yoghurt

Sources of Iron
Milk and milk products   none
Cereals and legumes   fortified flour and products**,
                                    fortified breakfast cereals, all legumes**

Meat and fish	red meats**, liver**
Fruit and vegetables	dark-green leafed vegetables
Other	molasses, chocolate and cocoa

Sources of Zinc

Milk and milk products	cheese
Cereals and legumes	all legumes, bread, wholemeal flour and products
Meat and fish	meat**, liver, crab and shellfish
Fruit and vegetables	very small amounts in most fruit and vegetables
Other	nuts

* also rich in iron
** particularly rich source

Fig 53   Sources of vitamins and minerals.

omit an important source of protein and calcium. Therefore, it is wise to eat from a wide variety of foods to prevent an excess of any one nutrient. Eating plenty of fruit and vegetables which are low in fat will help to balance the foods which are eaten which contain relatively high amounts of fat.

THE NEED FOR FLUID, ENERGY AND NUTRIENTS

Fluid

Our bodies are about 70 per cent water, so in a 70kg person 49kg is water. Cells (the constituents of every living thing) and blood need water in order to dissolve and carry nutrients. Water is also needed to cool the body and this is, of course, very important during exercise. Even a slight reduction in body water of 2 to 5 per cent (1.5–3.5l, 3–6pts) can cause a reduced efficiency in cellular function. People lose their powers of concentration and perform poorly overall. Dehydration does not allow the body sufficient water to cool itself and so the body may overheat. Fluid or water must be replaced. Fluid balance or hydration must therefore be

of prime importance to all sports people, including squash players.

Water is normally lost in three ways:

(i) Through the urine. This volume is increased by consuming certain nutrients such as alcohol (which has a diuretic effect).
(ii) Through the skin. This normally accounts for a small percentage, but during exercise can rise to over three litres per hour, depending on the intensity of exercise and the environmental conditions (high humidity inhibits loss and therefore you feel hotter).
(iii)   Through the lungs.

Water can also be lost abnormally in two ways:

(i) Through diarrhoea. This may be caused by infection or by eating too much fibre or large amounts of simple carbohydrate, which cannot be absorbed; they also cause water to be drawn into the gut from the body tissues (causing cell dehydration).
(ii) Through fevers. Extra water is lost through the skin in order to reduce body temperature.

Clearly, it is important to avoid extra fluid

loss. Be careful, though, as food and drink from dubious origins may be contaminated – even ice cubes made from impure water can cause infection. Knowing how much certain foods can be tolerated by your system (for example, dried fruits, which are both high in fibre and simple carbohydrates) is important. The amount which is tolerated can also be dependent on your circumstances. When apprehensive, some people suffer from loose bowel movements, thus increasing water loss.

Replacing the fluid lost during training and competition is vital. Our normal thirst 'mechanisms' often do not detect large losses. Therefore the level of loss during training sessions may not be replenished. Water losses need to be monitored actively; this means weighing yourself before and after any exercise. The change in weight will reflect the change in body-water content and hence the amount that needs replacing. This must be replaced. The best way to do this is to use a drink which is 'isotonic' to body fluids (the same concentration) or 'hypotonic' (weaker concentration). However, the drink should never be hypertonic (more concentrated) because body fluid will be drawn into the gut to dilute it. This causes (osmotic) diarrhoea and is counterproductive.

It has been found that a solution of: 2.5g of sugar per 100ml (about $^{1}/_{2}$oz per pint), 23mg of sodium (1.0mmol) per 100ml (a very small pinch per pint) and 20mg of potassium (0.5mmol) per 100ml, served cold (as from the fridge) in about half pint quantities is ideal. A dilute solution of orange squash (two to three tablespoons per pint) is just about the correct concentration. If using a commercially prepared drink, it is wise to check the concentration, which should not be greater than those given above. Plain water is also acceptable. Whatever is chosen it is important to consume an amount to replace the exact quantity lost.

Two pints weigh about 1kg (2lb) and are equivalent to about one litre; it takes some

practice and training to consume the amount lost during training sessions which can be as much as 3–4lb or more. Squash players need to be very vigilant.

A drink which contains alcohol causes extra urinary loss of water – it is a diuretic. Pints of beer will not do. Caffeine also has diuretic properties.

Finally, before competition it is helpful for players to prepare for the fluid which is to be lost. If you have carefully monitored losses during training and competitions you can predict how much you will lose. If you consume some fluid before the game to cover anticipated losses this can help you to maintain concentration and activity levels.

Requirements for Energy and Nutrients

The overall food and nutritional requirements of each player will depend on several factors including age, sex and body-weight (growing children or teenagers need proportionally greater amounts of food than adults while women need more iron than men, and men need more energy because they often weigh more), and duration and intensity of exercise undertaken. It is interesting that the amount of energy needed is the most variable and depends on the factors outlined above. The need for protein, minerals and vitamins is less variable.

ENERGY

Energy is derived from fat and carbohydrate (CHO) in food and, to a lesser extent, protein. The amount of energy in food is measured in units corresponding to the amount of heat that food would produce when it is 'burned' in the body. The heat produced can be thought of as providing the power to make the body work in much the same way as a coal fire produces heat to make steam to turn

Top New Zealand player for almost a decade – Ross Norman.

an engine. These units of 'heat' are calories.

A calorie is a very tiny amount of heat, and the amount in food is thousands of calories or kilocalories (kcal). Another unit which is used to measure the amount of energy in food is the joule – again a very tiny unit of 'work-energy' and so expressed in kilojoules (kJ). One kilocalorie is equivalent to 4.2 kilojoules (1kcal = 4.2kJ). Large amounts of kilojoules are expressed as megajoules (MJ); there are 1000kJ to a megajoule.

Energy in the food is used to do 'internal

British Under 23 and European Junior Champion – Cassie Jackman at full stretch.

work'; it keeps the heart beating and the lungs and other organs working, even when we are asleep. This basic, essential requirement for energy is known as the basal metabolic rate (BMR) and varies with body size. The BMR has the first priority for energy, however much is ingested.

The other basic needs for energy are in the renewal of body tissues and the excretion of waste products. Renewal of our body tissue takes place all the time but sometimes when exercising very hard, new muscle tissue is made. The amount of energy required to make about a pound of muscle tissue is thought to be about 5,000 to 7,000kcal (about 21 to 29.4MJ) above normal dietary intake.

After the energy needs for keeping the body 'ticking over' have been met, the rest of the energy supply can be put towards doing 'external' work or exercise. The amount of external work or exercise which can be undertaken can therefore be highly dependent upon just how much energy is left from the amount initially available. In some cases, where demands for exercise are allowed to override energy needs for basic maintenance or growth, people/children become thin, undernourished and underdeveloped.

SOURCES OF ENERGY

Carbohydrates as Dietary Sources of Energy

Plants store their energy as carbohydrate (CHO). This is a term used to cover a variety of molecules which all have similar chemical properties. Some molecules are small, taste sweet and are known as simple, or sugary, carbohydrate. They include glucose, sucrose (sugar), fructose, maltose and lactose (although lactose is an anomaly since animals produce it in milk for their young). Some molecules are large, do not taste sweet and are called complex, or starchy, carbohydrate (the starches in bread, potatoes, rice and pasta are either starchy or complex). Finally there are some forms of carbohydrate which we cannot digest or absorb and are known as unavailable carbohydrate or dietary fibre. Eventually *all* dietary sources of the sugary and starchy carbohydrate, sometimes collectively called available CHO, will be transformed into glucose and carried to the cells by the blood.

Each gram of available CHO provides 4kcal of energy to the body. It is found in all foods of plant origin: cereals, fruit, vegetables (including pulses such as dried peas, beans and lentils) and to a limited extent in nuts (*see* Fig 52). Fruit and vegetables contain a very high percentage of water and so the carbohydrate which is present is considerably diluted. For this reason these foods are less 'energy-dense'; this also applies to other nutrients which are similarily diluted. It also means that to consume a large amount of energy a great quantity of these foods need to be eaten. This is useful for slimmers, but not necessarily for the person who requires a high energy intake in a hurry. However, foods made from cereal grains (bread, pasta and biscuits or cakes and so on) do not contain as much water and so are more energy-dense. Bread, breakfast cereals, pasta and rice are all rich sources of CHO and are relatively energy-dense.

Once the CHO is consumed it appears in the blood as glucose. This can be used directly for energy or stored in the muscle or liver as glycogen, the 'animal equivalent' of starch – a very important source of energy for all animal cells. There is a finite amount of glycogen which can be stored, about 200g (7oz). The glycogen stored in the muscle probably determines the amount of work which can be done by that muscle, while any excess glucose is then made into fat and stored in the adipose tissue.

Fats as Dietary Sources of Energy

Fat is found in almost all foods, since it is an important part of the cell wall of all plant and animal tissue. Plants do not store energy as fat (except in nuts) so the amount of fat in plant sources of food will be very low. Animals, including humans, store energy in their bodies as fat, indeed an average woman may have 10kg (22lb) of fat in her body. This fat is stored in many places: in adipose tissue around vital organs, under the skin and amongst muscle fibres. Therefore meat or animal products such as eggs, milk and milk products all contain fat, often in significant amounts (see Fig 52).

Fat is energy-dense and supplies 9kcal per gram, more than twice as much per unit weight as CHO. Animal products do not contain as much water as fruit and vegetables and so are much more energy- and nutrient-dense. Fat can also taste nice: think of the taste of fried mushrooms compared to boiled or the taste of buttered rather than dry toast. Eating fat is easy and because it is energy-dense it provides energy in small amounts of food; hence overindulgence is easy. Active and busy players need this form of energy which can be eaten in a hurry, but the slimmer needs to be careful.

Sources of Energy in the Diet and Long-Term Health

The amount and type of food-energy we consume may influence our health. It is generally agreed that there is a weight–height ratio at which adults are fitter and less prone to develop various life-threatening diseases. The more fat you carry, the higher will be the ratio and the higher the risk of such diseases occurring. A simple way to calculate whether your weight–height ratio is satisfactory is to use this internationally accepted method: weight (kg) divided by height (m) squared. This is termed the body mass index (BMI). The range thought to be acceptable is 17–25. If your BMI is below the bottom end, this is just as disturbing as if it is too high. Lean people may be more agile and active around the court but if weight is reduced too far, this indicates poor body reserves of nutrients because of a restrictive dietary intake. A very restrictive intake can lead to nutrient deficiencies which will ultimately affect performance.

This weight–height ratio (BMI) is a simple and quick test; however, it does not tell us how much of an individual is fat and how much is lean (muscle) tissue. To find out the ratio of fat to lean tissue a more specific measurement has to be made. One method which can be used is based on the assumption that the fat under the skin is a fair reflection of total body fat. Using special, skinfold callipers (see Fig 54), the amount of fat under the skin can be assessed. The total body fat can then be estimated by using a formula (Eisenman and Johnson, 1982). Women, for physiological reasons, have a higher percentage of body fat than men. The amount of fat which different people have varies and

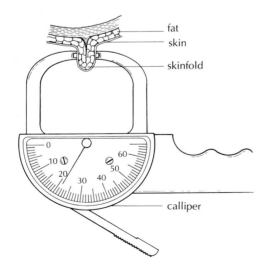

Fig 54   Estimating body fat with skinfold callipers.

can be manipulated by use of exercise and diet. However, the difference between men and women always remains. A list of measured body fats is given below:

Average adult man (20–50 years)
    15–25 per cent fat
Average adult female (20–50 years)
    26–35 per cent fat

Adult male tennis player
    about 16 per cent fat
Adult female tennis player
    about 20 per cent fat

Adult male distance runner
    6–13 per cent fat
Adult female distance runner
    15–19 per cent fat

Adult male squash player
    about 19 per cent fat
Adult female squash player
    about 23 per cent fat

The type of 'energy' consumed may have an effect on long-term health. It is thought advisable to consume the majority of energy in the form of carbohydrate. Sugary carbohydrate can cause dental disease and therefore reliance should be on the complex, or starchy, carbohydrate. Fat is thought to be associated with heart disease and certain forms of cancer and for these reasons it is best avoided in large amounts. The saturated fats found in animal sources are thought to be more harmful than the fats from vegetable sources which are largely unsaturated.

The development of certain diseases which mainly afflict people in the developed countries is probably due to a number of factors; two of these are diet and lack of exercise. At this time it is difficult to say how 'protective' exercise will be in the long term, especially that practised by amateur and professional sports people. Certainly it is important to meet energy and food needs, and this may mean a higher fat intake than would ordinarily be advised.

PROTEIN

The requirement for dietary protein depends on several factors including: the amount of muscle tissue present (as there is more body protein, there is more to maintain and replace); the amount of new tissue synthesis (in the growth phase proportionally more protein is required plus the increased demand for energy to synthesise it); the amount of fractions of protein lost through sweat and hair/skin.

Much controversy surrounds the nature and extent of the body's need for protein. The body can become very efficient at conserving its store of protein which is found in every cell in the body. It would seem that squash players need the same amount of protein per kilogram of body-weight as untrained individuals, although they will need more if energy supplies are not sufficient to meet demand, since protein can be used as a source of energy. This is very wasteful because once it is used for energy, it cannot be used for body protein 'repair'.

It is not surprising, therefore, that there is a close relationship between protein and energy requirements. If enough carbohydrate and fat are consumed to supply energy, sports people need no more protein than anyone else. Yet some players take supplementary protein. Unfortunately this form of protein, unlike that found in normal foods, does not have fat or carbohydrate. Therefore, the energy supply may be less than needed and the protein can be wasted. Work currently in progress at Leeds Polytechnic (unpublished) tends to indicate that the consumption of protein supplements can actually cause some sports players to reduce their overall food intake. This is clearly counterproductive in terms of maintaining an adequate energy and nutrient supply. Finally, protein will only be used to build new tissue if there is an appropriate training programme. Of course, you need plenty of energy to maintain training so the argument once again revolves around the need for, and high priority of, energy foods in the diet.

Amino acids are the tiny molecules which are joined together in particular sequences to make proteins. Proteins in hair will have a different sequence to the proteins in muscle (which is why hair and muscle look so different). Once again, all proteins contain all amino acids but in different amounts, depending on source and function. Generally, proteins from animal sources are nearer in amino-acid pattern and proportion to our own bodies and our needs. However, it is possible to get all these amino acids from plant sources. Vegetarians do this and are perfectly healthy. So it is quite possible to get all the amino acids and protein from the cheaper vegetable sources of protein such as baked beans. By mixing foods together a better mix of amino acids is ensured. Putting cereals (bread, pasta, rice) together with nuts or pulses (dried beans, peas or lentils) creates a perfect complement of amino acids, precisely the same as that found in the best sirloin steak.

How Much Protein?

The actual amount of protein needed per person is difficult to define. It is possible to give values for grams of protein, but this is meaningless unless it is put into the context of food. Values for adults of between 1–2g protein per kg of body-weight per day have been quoted. For someone who weighs 80kg the need for protein could be estimated at 80–160g per day. The values given in the Department of Health and Social Security's recommended intake tables are comparable to this. About 40kcal of energy are required per gram of protein. In the above example

this would mean a food energy intake of between 3,200 and 6,400 kcal per day.

Food, however, is a mixture of nutrients and if the food in the diet provides, say, 3,000kcal, this amount is likely to contain at least 80g of protein or probably a lot more. It is very difficult to consume too little protein when eating a variety of foods (see Fig 52 – it shows some sources of protein).

MINERALS AND VITAMINS

There is also little evidence to suggest that athletes have a greater bodily demand for vitamins compared to non-athletes. As has been said, food is a mixture of nutrients and as food intake rises (as it must do to support activity) so does the level of vitamin supply through the food. A very bizarre diet indeed would have to be chosen for any deficiency to occur. However, it is possible to over-indulge in vitamin supplements – and this can be dangerous. It is becoming apparent that not only can over-indulging in vitamins (even vitamin C) lead to the development of harmful conditions, but also that such supplements affect the absorption of other nutrients. Individuals should take care and, if supplements are thought to be necessary, they should first seek medical advice to confirm a positive need.

Minerals may be thought of in two groups: those which we require in relatively large amounts and those which we require in trace amounts. The former, which are of importance here, are sodium, potassium and calcium. Of those required in very small amounts the most important is iron. Sodium and potassium loss in sweat barely reach levels whereby supplements are required above normal dietary intake and therefore they should not be considered outside the context of a normal varied diet.

There is, however, perhaps slightly more concern over adequate iron intake in athletes

Liz Irving looks likely to be left stranded with this forehand boast from British Open Champion Susan Devoy.

due to the occasional occurrence of the condition known as 'sports anaemia', although it has not been ascribed to squash players. The reason for this anaemia is not fully understood but may be a result of physical stress on the red blood cells or from abnormal losses of blood – both due to the intensity and prolonged effort of training and exercise. If anaemia is diagnosed, iron supplements will need to be taken. It would also be wise to make sure the diet contains iron-rich foods (*see* Fig 53).

A more serious cause of concern is the sportswoman (and it usually is the female) who deliberately restricts food intake to slim. When food is restricted the supply of nutrients is reduced overall. This is especially critical with respect to iron and calcium,

both of which are crucial to health in the long and short term. Women who exercise hard and who limit their diet compensate for inadequate dietary supplies of iron by ceasing to menstruate. This is an indication that hormonal changes have occurred which are not normal.

The other system which these changes affect is the synthesis and resynthesis of bone. On a low calcium intake (poor dietary supply) where some hormonal levels are low, bone is not effectively calcified and a condition known as osteoporosis occurs. Any exercise which is isometric in nature, so that it puts a strain on the long bones, helps to counteract this process to an extent. However, the disturbing feature is that it is not known how the damage will manifest itself once serious sport is stopped. Women, in particular, should pay attention to their overall food intake and to their calcium and iron. Again, if the food-energy in a varied diet is in excess of 2,000kcal there should be no problem in meeting the needs for iron and calcium. Fig 53 also shows sources of calcium and other vitamins in the diet.

Overall, the athlete who is not restricting intake should not need any vitamin or mineral supplements. In any event, supplements should only be commenced after a deficiency has been confirmed.

TRAINING SCHEDULES AND FOOD FOR COMPETITIONS

Rest periods are a vital part of successful training and allow the player to replenish energy and nutrient stores. Any schedule must, of course, allow time for the preparation and consumption of food. Obviously, without food we simply do not have the energy available to perform and it must therefore be an essential part of the training schedule. Indeed, it may well be that relaxation periods should become eating periods. 'Tapering' of exercise before competition allows for just this repletion phase. Productivity of training might well be improved if coaches and players were to give more thought to rest and food periods.

Timing of meals should be arranged so that the major part of digestion is complete before activity commences. Fat and protein foods on the whole, take longer to move through the stomach and small intestine (two to four hours). Carbohydrate and cold foods are much quicker (one to two hours, depending on the size of the meal). Sportsmen and women need to eat after a training session and good anticipation of food needs is essential. As it may not always be possible to consume a full meal, it is sensible to take your own food (i.e. some sandwiches and a flask

of fluid to provide the essential nutrient and fluid replacement). If you do have to eat out, carbohydrate in the form of baked potatoes, pizza or pasta are the most sensible foods – meals and snacks should always be based around the starchy carbohydrates, since they are more effective at repleting glycogen stores lost during competition or training sessions.

TRAINING FOR SQUASH

Training for squash, primarily a sport performed under aerobic conditions, mainly aims to enhance the cardiovascular system and muscle. This ensures efficient and continuous supply of 'fuel' and oxygen to the working muscles for a long period. Training sessions at sub-maximal work load – aerobic training – also condition the body to use its fat stores as the major fuel. This is important, especially under match conditions as the store of fat in the body is much greater than CHO and will therefore last for longer. However, fat is not the sole fuel and some CHO must also be used; this usage becomes proportionally greater as the intensity of the exercise increases – usually towards the end of a match or training session. It is the reserve of stored CHO present at this time that will determine the duration of intense work. For training sessions that are longer than an hour the amount of stored CHO (glycogen) determines the intensity of the work that the muscles can do. Power becomes increasingly difficult to generate in muscles that have diminishing amounts of available glycogen.

Squash players not only need stamina to see them through a long match but also the strength for 'explosive' bursts of energy. These bursts demand an anaerobic metabolism when the only fuel source is glucose (glycogen). Training sessions therefore aim both to build muscles and to train them to work and tolerate anaerobic conditions. Each exercise will normally be carried out to exhaustion; this conditions the muscles to anaerobic metabolism and by its nature depletes glycogen.

Training also seems to effect a change in the efficiency with which muscles store glycogen; it has been observed that training brings about swift, efficient repletion of stores, but only if muscles have a plentiful dietary supply. Generally, however, starchy carbohydrate may well be better at replacing the lost glycogen.

Aerobic conditioning means long training sessions which are also expensive in terms of energy usage; it is therefore essential to eat properly during this training. Concentrated sources of CHO are important (*see* Fig 52) as well as high energy foods (containing fat) such as chocolate, rich cakes, nuts and biscuits. Fortified drinks or soups are also useful, e.g. using milk and adding sugar and cream. Nor should you forget to replace the fluids which will have been lost in vigorous training.

Squash players may also need to consider their lean–fat ratio. The consideration of carrying excess body fat is an important part of training but it is vital that the level of body fat is steadily maintained. Constant dieting does little to afford you energy for effective training.

Competition

As competition time approaches, the will to win must be combined with the suggested training programme. Diet can have a role to play in this, but food eaten immediately before competition has little effect on performance; it can in fact be detrimental. It is rather the extended period of preparation, including training and diet, which will affect performance on the day. Unlike food, however, it is imperative to drink before a game since lack of fluids – dehydration – may prevent you even finishing.

How to Arrive Ready to Compete

The message of this chapter has been to ensure that you get the 'energy books balanced', which means ensuring that energy is replaced in the working muscle. If this becomes part of the training schedule, relaxing before the event allows the body muscles to recoup their energy reserves quite naturally; that is to say, you should taper your training schedule.

In fact, it can be unproductive to follow an unusually high carbohydrate diet for several days before the event, as this can lead to discomfort and diarrhoea. By careful measurement of a player's food intake it has been shown how very difficult it is for the individual actually to judge by how much food intake is increasing. More often than not CHO intake is raised but the contribution to energy intake from fat is lowered. This means an overall lowering of energy intake. So instead of the carbohydrate being stored, it may be used for the essential work of body maintenance (so that glycogen storage is less than expected). The message here is that if good dietary habits are developed to support training, they will also be highly suitable for immediate preparation for a game (which is often of shorter duration than the training sessions).

The planning of meals and snacks before a competition also needs consideration. As already mentioned, it is important to have the intestine as free as possible from the process of digestion; meals should therefore be finished at least two hours (preferably four hours) before playing, since the anticipation of competition may reduce intestinal function. Players should carefully plan those meals which they *feel* will be most beneficial – remember the psychological value of foods.

The content of the meals is largely irrelevant in terms of providing energy (this has already been stored). Sugary snacks should be avoided as these may delay the release of internal energy (*see* below). It would also be wise to avoid those foods which are known to produce flatulence as this can be very uncomfortable during a game.

The amount of energy available to the working muscles during a game can of course be crucial to the outcome. The type of training will determine how the individual responds to the demands of the exercise; if the training has been to support aerobic metabolism, fat is predominantly burned, sparing glycogen. Therefore, glycogen is available for all-out effort at the end of the game. However, there are other factors which can also help or hinder.

If something sugary is taken about forty-five minutes before starting a game, the body will be caught out and will not react as well to exercise. The body will be expecting to store food/nutrients and not to mobilise fuel. The hormones which act to control body chemistry will not promote energy release and this can be very unfortunate for the player.

However, if something sugary is taken once the game is started then this glucose is used by the muscles. Now it is not possible to stop in the middle of a game to take a sugary drink or food, but during rest periods you should replace some of the glucose which has inevitably been used by the muscles during play.

Some ergogenic (or exercise-enhancing) aids may also be tried to encourage effective use of the fuel supplies. One of these which can be useful, provided it is not misused by over-indulgence, is caffeine. Consumed about forty-five minutes before exercise it has two effects: it is a stimulant and reduces the subjective feeling of effort and it causes fatty acids to be 'mobilised' and used as fuel, so sparing glycogen.

The amount of caffeine which has been found to produce this effect is 4mg per kg of body-weight. Caffeine is found in chocolate to a small extent and in drinks in the following amounts:

1 cup (200ml) cola		35mg
1 cup (150ml) coffee, instant		70mg
	percolated	120mg
	filter	160mg
1 cup (150ml) tea		50mg

Caffeine is a drug. If it is given in large and uncontrolled amounts it can produce vascular changes which are harmful. In addition, at everyday doses it can have a pronounced diuretic effect which is undesirable when hydration is required.

Indeed, hydration is probably the single most important factor for success on the day. It is essential that fluid is replaced as often as possible throughout the sets of games. The concept of fluid with a suitable concentration, to ensure maximum absorption, has been discussed earlier but remember it may help to supplement with some sugar and glucose during competition.

Eating between games should follow the same basic rules and be completed at least two hours before the next. Some digestion and absorption of food does occur at submaximal levels of exercise. Each individual should note the types of food that can be easily consumed between games and which to avoid.

Summary

Eating for a serious squash player should be taken just as seriously as the training schedule and should be part of it. Food provides the fuel for play and the nutrients to keep the body healthy. To ignore these basic facts is to jeopardise success at your sport. Limiting food or not planning meals can be counterproductive. The monitoring of both food intake and body-weight should be part of the squash player's routine.

4   Injury Prevention

CLASSIFICATION OF INJURY

In order to prevent injuries it is preferable to understand why they occur and where they occur in the body. An injury may be due to an external force (extrinsic injury) or to a force within the body (intrinsic injury). Extrinsic injuries happen when a player collides with an object such as the wall, the ground, a piece of equipment in the gym or even another player. They can also be caused by an object hitting the body, such as a racket. Intrinsic injuries may happen without any particular cause (incidental injury) but are more likely to occur when the training load is rapidly increased in intensity and frequency (overuse injury). Most injuries tend to occur quite suddenly (acute injury) but fortunately tend to settle very quickly. However, acute injuries may progress and become chronic injuries – these are usually more difficult to treat and take longer to overcome. You are far more likely to get injured towards the end of a training session or match, when you become tired, than at any other time, so take more care as you become fatigued.

SITE OF INJURY

Sports injuries may occur anywhere in the body, such as in muscles, tendons (pullies attached to the bone from the muscles), tenosynovia (the protective sheaths around a tendon), ligaments (fibrous bands joining two bones together at a joint), joints and bones. It is helpful to grade the injuries into three groups:

(i)   Group A   Minimal damage when only bruising occurs and there is no major disruption to the muscle, tendon, ligament or whatever. Small blood vessels are damaged, however, and leak blood which forms a bruise (haematoma).

(ii)   Group B   Some disruption of the tissues takes place and a sprain, strain, partial tear or partial rupture takes place in a muscle, tendon (tendonitis) tendon sheath (tenosynovitis), ligament or bone (stress fracture). Stress fractures of bones can be likened to the cracks in a piece of wire which has been repeatedly bent – at first the wire looks strong but eventually, if stressed enough, it can break right through.

(iii)   Group C   Complete ruptures of muscles, tendons and ligaments, fractured or broken bones and dislocated joints.

Further classification of injury can be as shown below:

Extrinsic (outside force)
    collisions
    falls
    equipment

Intrinsic (internal force)
    incidental (no cause)
    overuse
    acute
    chronic

AVOIDANCE OF INJURIES

The basic rule for avoiding injury is to increase your own fitness through increased speed, strength, endurance and flexibility, as outlined in Chapter 2. Using the training programme in a sensible progressive way reduces the chances of sustaining intrinsic and overuse injuries. Skill is not only important in making a better all-round player but also enables the player to avoid injury through inappropriate technique. It is important to teach and practise good techniques, both on and off the court. For example tennis elbow, which is an inflammation of the muscle attachment on the outside of the elbow, may be due to the squash player holding the racket handle too tightly. It may, however, be due to the racket handle either being too small or too big for a particular player.

Warm-up and Cool-down

A warm-up is essential not only in preparation for matches but also in training. By gradually increasing the intensity of work and building up the number of skills to be rehearsed, the body and mind are both being warmed up (*see* Chapter 2). The muscles are controlled by electrical impulses fed to them from the brain and this system needs tuning and adjusting – just as the muscles need

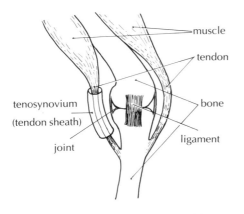

Fig 55 Physiological representation of the knee.

warming up. Equally important is the cool-down, when more emphasis is put on flexibility in order to test for any minor injury that may have occurred during exercise.

Gentle rhythmic movement also helps to flush out the waste products of metabolism from the muscles that have built up during high-intensity exercise. Muscle stiffness the following day may be reduced by performing a regular post-match or post-training drill of stretching and low-intensity exercise (*see* Chapter 2).

Protection

Most extrinsic injuries can be avoided by taking sensible precautions and checking the safety of the training venue and any equipment that is used in it. Gyms should be well ventilated, well lit and with any sharp edges, radiators or walls padded with foam. Doors and windows should be secured and other recreational equipment stored correctly and well out of the way of the training area.

The squash court must be checked before each match or training session. The floor should be clean and swept for dust and loose particles that may have accumulated. The court may be slippery from sweat or water dropped on the court or rainwater which may have leaked through a faulty roof. The court door must be well fitting and the door handle should sit flush with the surface of the door. The walls and tin line need checking to see that no loose jagged edges are protruding.

People who have to wear spectacles or contact lenses must use shatter-proof lenses or soft contacts. All players should be encouraged to wear protective plastic spectacle frames to protect their eyes from the ball which unfortunately fits into the eye socket and can cause serious eye injuries.

The use of carbon-fibre rackets, particularly the all-in-one variety, may produce more injuries in the forearm, such as tennis elbow. More resilient materials will dissipate some of the shock waves, reducing the energy transmitted up through the handle to the arm. Tennis-elbow splints or straps, if worn regularly by those people susceptible to this particular injury, may enable them to continue playing without further discomfort.

Shoes should be well fitting; wear new shoes for short periods in training only until they feel comfortable, in order to cut down on blisters. Make sure you choose the right footwear for the right surface. You may need to have different pairs for artificial surfaces and for wooden floors in the courts and in gymnasiums when training. Always remove dentures and on no account chew gum when either training or playing in case you choke on it when injured.

Some players may wish to strap their fingers, ankles or feet, particularly if they have been injured in the past. The strapping needs to be inelastic, such as zinc oxide, in order to support joints adequately, and must be removed after exercise allowing a full range of movement to take place. A trained physiotherapist can show you how to apply the tape.

Self-control

The rules of the game and the regulations controlling the use of training venues have been devised not only to ensure fair play but also to prevent injury; it is therefore prudent to observe these rules for your own safety. It is especially important to play with and against people of your own physique and standard of play.

Self-control plays an important role in preventing and reducing injury. Try to organise your day so that there is adequate time for meals, allowing at least two hours to elapse after a large meal before training. Most athletes need a minimum of eight hours' sleep each night and time must also be allocated for training, eating, studying or working. Fatigue will set in if not enough

time is allowed for adequate rest between training sessions and this is the biggest cause of most sports injuries as well as skill breakdown. Regular showering or bathing after training and frequent washing of kit will help reduce the incidence of fungal infections of the skin. Do not borrow other people's clothing or towels and make sure you always have clean, dry clothing to change into after a training session. Athletes should be non-smokers, not only for obvious health reasons but also because the nicotine in cigarettes attaches itself to the oxygen-carrying component of the red blood cells (haemoglobin), thus reducing the available space for oxygen to be transported to the muscles. This effect lasts for up to three weeks after the last cigarette has been smoked.

Alcohol should never be consumed before a match or training session – not only to avoid errors of judgement but also because alcohol dehydrates the body and makes it perform less efficiently. After a hard match or training session, particularly in hot conditions, plain fluid should be drunk first before racing to the bar.

Check-list for Injury Prevention

(i) Environment; clothes; shoes; equipment; surfaces; protective spectacle frames.
(ii) Control: training/game rules; physique; tactics.
(iii) Fitness: skill; strength; speed; endurance; flexibility.
(iv) Self-discipline: warm up; diet; sleep; smoking; hygiene; alcohol.

MEDICAL PROBLEMS

Frequently it may be illness and not injury that prevents the sports person from training. Any squash player who has an infection, such as a heavy cold, a chest infection or flu, should not train or play, especially if the body

Martine Le Moignan – winner of the World Championship 1989.

temperature is elevated above normal (36.9°C, 98.4°F) or if the resting pulse rate is appreciably higher than normal. You will not be able to perform well and certainly will not get any beneficial training effect if you continue to train at this stage; you also run the risk of the infection getting worse and the heart muscle being affected (myocarditis). Rest is essential until the illness passes. Low-grade chronic infections of the teeth, skin or sinuses for example, may prevent you performing at peak level, and treatment should be sought earlier rather than later. Some virus infections, such as glandular fever, may linger on for weeks and regrettably there is no treatment – so you must remain patient until the illness passes, returning gradually to full training.

Dehydration

A reduction in body-weight of 1 per cent through lost sweat results in a 10 per cent reduction in work capacity, likewise, a 2 per cent loss will result in a 20 per cent reduction. It is therefore vital that any sweat lost is adequately and promptly replaced by water, not only to enhance performance but also to prevent injury. Some people (particularly when training regularly on hot courts, gyms or at the end of summer) may become chronically dehydrated with a subsequent reduction in body-weight, reduced urine output and a rise in the resting pulse. Regular weighing and checking of the volume and colour of the urine should ensure that dehydration does not become a problem – thirst alone is not a reliable indicator of dehydration.

OVERTRAINING

This condition is difficult to spot and may creep up on the player and coach without either being aware of what is happening. It usually occurs when the player increases the

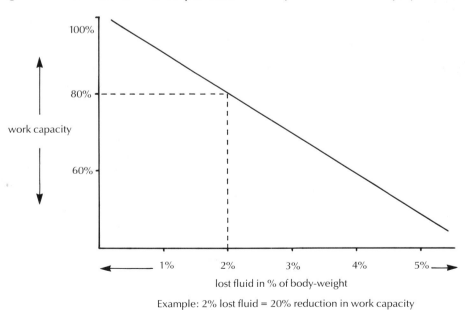

Example: 2% lost fluid = 20% reduction in work capacity

Fig 56 The relationship between the loss of body fluid and reduction in work capacity.

training load both in frequency and intensity, not allowing enough time to eat, sleep, study or work. As the performance drops off the athlete tries to compensate by increasing the training load, only to suffer further deterioration in performance, starting down the slippery slope and getting involved in a vicious cycle of increased work and poor performance. The only cure is to rest for four days and increase both the fluid and carbohydrate intake, resisting the temptation to restart training after only one or two days when feeling a little recovered.

WOMEN

Women who have frequent heavy periods may lose enough iron to make themselves anaemic. When anaemia occurs the red blood cells are unable to carry sufficient oxygen to the muscles, resulting in tiredness both on and off the court. The doctor can easily correct this deficiency and advice should be sought as early as possible. Some women who undergo a lot of endurance training may cease to have any periods, particularly if they reduce their body fat. This condition is known as amenorrhoea and is quite normal in these circumstances; periods will return when the training load is decreased. Pregnant women can safely continue to train until they start feeling uncomfortable, indeed, regular exercise in pregnancy results in healthier babies and easier childbirth for the mother. Playing competitive games after the first 3–4 months of pregnancy is best avoided to decrease the risk of miscarriage due to body contact.

CHILDREN

Bones continue to grow up to the age of about eighteen in males and about sixteen in females. However, during growth the bones are not strong enough for the muscles and tendons attached to them, so heavy weight training and repetitive high-load training should not be performed by pre-pubertal children. In some children the points at which tendons are attached to bones become inflamed, swollen and tender. This may happen just below the knee (Osgood-Schlatter's condition) or at the back of the heel (Sever's condition). Boys of twelve to fourteen years and girls between ten to twelve develop Osgood-Schlatter's; it is indicated by pain just below the knee while vigorously extending the knee. They should be allowed to continue to play but should avoid long hard sessions. The only treatment is to reduce the loading to that particular point, by cutting down on the training until the condition settles. The child can train on resilient surfaces such as grass during training, and, when playing squash, the use of shock absorbing heel inserts made of sorbothane will prove effective in relieving pain. Children develop power and explosive force after puberty and so power-training should not be undertaken until after this time. Training with very light weights will, however, help with the technical skills of heavier weight-training later on.

VETERANS

Older sports people are not especially prone to particular injuries, but as age advances the chance of their being injured increases and the longer it takes them to recover from injury. If you go back to squash later in life, having had a few years away from the sport, start gently with a gradual increase in the frequency and intensity of each session. Secondary injuries may occur in joints previously damaged in earlier years; for example, an injury such as osteoarthritis of the knee joint may develop long after a torn cartilage has been removed. These secondary injuries may prevent you from doing as much training as you would like, but you will have to adjust to this, perhaps supplementing your usual training with swimming and cycling.

Squash players who have previously played at a high level, for example County standard, may stand a bigger risk of collapsing on court from a heart attack if they go back to playing after several years without a gradual build-up in fitness. They still retain the ability to push themselves to the limit but they forget that their cardiovascular fitness and musculoskeletal fitness are not as they used to be.

TRAVEL

When travelling away from home, whether abroad or in your own country, you may experience difficulty in sleeping, especially during the first few nights. A mild sleeping-pill may prove helpful at this time and your doctor should be able to help if insomnia becomes a problem. Stay clear of new and untried exotic foods, keep to your usual diet if at all possible and wash any fruit and salads in *clean* water before eating them. Check that the water supply is safe to drink and, if not, consume bottled water only. When going to a hot climate the body takes ten days or so to acclimatise to the heat. After this period the salt content of the sweat is reduced and stabilised so all that is required is a little extra salt during the first few days, although you should not take salt tablets as they can make you feel ill.

If you have a fair skin, you should keep out of the sun and, even if you tan easily, you should still avoid sunbathing as you may become dehydrated. Ideally you should always wear long sleeves and long trousers at dusk and at dawn to avoid insect bites, and try to use plenty of insect repellent. Check with your doctor – well in advance of your trip – to find out whether any special vaccinations are required. A travel check-list will include: vaccinations, food, water, heat acclimatisation, sleep disturbance and jet lag.

DOPING

It is your responsibility as a player to ensure that you do not abuse the drug-testing regulations, either intentionally or by error. Mistakes can occur when over-the-counter pain killers, cough mixtures, anti-diarrhoea medicines and nasal congestants are used which may contain small amounts of codeine and ephedrine. Both drugs are on the banned list and will show up in urine as positive in a dope test. Check with the governing body or the Sports Council's Drugs Advisory Group for an up-to-date list of drugs you can and cannot take.

FIRST AID

Resuscitation

If you are a coach you have a responsibility to know the basic procedures of resuscitation. When a serious casualty occurs your first aim is to save life before worrying about the extent of any sports injury:

(i)   Check the airway and remove any object which might be preventing air entering the lungs; remove any false teeth, clear the mouth of vomit or chewing gum and loosen any clothing around the throat. Extend the neck fully in order to prevent the tongue flopping down against the back of the throat.

(ii)   Check that the casualty is now breathing; if not, start CPR (cardiopulmonary resuscitation) by giving the kiss of life. Breathe into the mouth of the casualty at the same time as pinching his nose to prevent air escaping from it.

(iii) Check the circulation by feeling for a pulse; if you cannot detect it, start compressing the chest wall firmly four times for each of your breaths until the casualty starts breathing and regains his pulse, or until the ambulance arrives.

(iv) After the patient has regained consciousness or started breathing by himself, check for any bleeding. If there is bleeding, apply firm pressure with a gauze swab or handkerchief for five minutes (in most cases this will be sufficient to stop blood loss from major vessels). You can then start assessing the extent of any injury and try to relieve pain by placing the casualty in a stable position on his side, and splinting any obvious fractures. Ideally you should also have checked beforehand where the nearest telephone is; you must send someone to summon the ambulance in order to evacuate the injured person.

First-Aid Box

Your first-aid box must contain: crêpe bandages, gauze squares, zinc-oxide tape, elastoplasts, cotton wool, triangular bandage, scissors, antiseptic solution and analgesic (pain killing) tablets.

Treatment of Sports Injuries

The aim of treatment is to reduce the amount of damage already done, relieve pain and promote healing. When a sports injury or soft tissue injury occurs, small blood vessels

Australian no. 1 Chris Dittmar showing an excellent low, balanced position to play a forehand drop shot.

become torn and blood escapes causing bruising and swelling. Action should be taken to help reduce the amount of blood escaping and so cut down on the size of the swelling, both of which hinder repair and rehabilitation. A mnemonic (RICE) is useful in this context:

Rest
Ice
Compression
Elevation

Rest is required for the first twenty-four hours following an injury in order to prevent further bleeding.

Ice is applied to the injury for ten minutes every two hours in the first twenty-four hours. This reduces pain, swelling and further bleeding. The ice should be wrapped in a damp tea-towel and must not come into direct contact with the skin; if it does, an ice burn may occur. If ice is not available, cold water from the tap will suffice, as will a bag of frozen peas from the freezer!

Compression of the injury by a firmly applied crêpe bandage prevents further blood loss and reduces the size of any swelling. The bandage should not be too tight and you may need to re-apply the crêpe in the first twenty-four hours if it becomes too loose or too tight.

Elevation assists in the 'drainage' of swelling and the prevention of further loss of blood. The affected limb should be raised above the level of the heart for twenty-four hours.

Treatment of Blisters

The treatment for a blister depends upon whether or not the skin overlying it is intact. If it is, the blister should be left alone, but, if the skin has been broken the blister should be 'deroofed' with a clean pair of scissors. This prevents infection setting in and also assists in the blister bed healing more rapidly, if perhaps a little more uncomfortably in the short term. While training, the blister should be covered with a dry, non-absorbent dressing held in place by a piece of tape or strapping.

Rehabilitation

Early rehabilitation of most injuries should be encouraged in order to shorten the time taken to reach a full recovery. In the first twenty-four hours when 'RICE' is applied, gentle passive movements are made to assist in the drainage of any swelling and to prevent blood clots forming in the deep veins. After a further twenty-four hours, more active stretching exercises are performed followed by strengthening exercises. The muscles around an injury rapidly lose power and the co-ordination of muscle movements also worsens within a few hours of the injury being sustained. As the muscles regain power, re-education of squash skills becomes a priority, eventually allowing a return to training and to playing matches.

Models for Rehabilitation

(i) **Group A injuries**
Bruising only has occurred and all that is generally required is the application of RICE in the first twenty-four hours, followed by a fairly rapid resumption of normal training.

(ii) **Group B injuries**
(a) Ligaments/joints. A sprained ligament on the outside of the ankle joint is one of the more common squash injuries. The principies used for the rehabilitation of this particular injury may also be applied to similar injuries that occur in other parts of the body.

After the first twenty-four hours (when RICE is applied) you should try to walk on the injured side without a limp in order to stretch any scar tissue that is forming into its correct anatomical alignment. Initially this may mean that you will have to walk very slowly, before progressing first to normal walking pace and then to walking and jogging on grass five to ten metres at a time, slowly increasing the distance to twenty-five, fifty, seventy-five and then one hundred metres. When you have reached this stage, continue jogging for up to four hundred metres before starting a few sprints of five to ten metres, followed by sprints of twenty-five, fifty, seventy-five and one hundred metres. Now run backwards and start weaving and jumping to strengthen the ankle further.

Nerves are damaged in a ligament injury and so lose their ability to tell the brain where in space the foot is. These nerves need to be re-educated and the best way to do so is by balance exercises. These positional or 'proprioceptive' exercises must be done at the same time as the stretching and strengthening drills. Start by trying to 'stork-stand' on your injured leg and then close your eyes. After this, try throwing a tennis ball up into the air and catching it again while balancing on one leg. The degree of difficulty can be increased by standing on a balance or wobble board. When you can do all of this quite happily for fifteen to twenty minutes you are then fit enough to resume normal training. However, if having done this your ankle still doesn't feel stable or if you are unable to play, you should seek advice from a sports clinic or qualified physiotherapist.
(b) Muscles and tendons. The aim of the rehabilitation is to prevent shortening of the muscle or tendon by inappropriate scar tissue formation. Scar tissue may contract for several weeks after an injury.

Following the usual RICE application in the first twenty-four hours you should gently stretch the injured muscle for ten minutes each morning and evening and for a minute every hour during the day. As gentle stretching becomes less uncomfortable, more active stretching and static strengthening exercises should be undertaken, followed by dynamic exercises with increased loadings. For example, with a torn quadriceps muscle (thigh) start with straight-leg exercises, then continue by bending the knee and follow up by attaching weights of one to two kilograms to the ankle while bending and straightening the knee.

After this, the routine of jogging, sprinting, weaving, running backwards together with balance exercises, as used for the ankle injury, should be followed.

(iii) Group C injuries

Bone fractures and dislocated joints. Most fractures or broken bones, together with joint dislocations, are major injuries and will need a minimum of six weeks' immobilisation before any rehabilitation can commence. They also require close medical supervision. Stress fractures, however, need only be rested for three weeks before gentle progressive training is resumed. If you think you have a stress fracture you should stop training and seek medical advice.

5   Mental Training

WHAT IS IN IT FOR ME?

Mental problems are apparent at all levels in sport. Indeed, the ability to cope with psychological pressures may be the main selective factor in deciding who makes it to the top. Unfortunately there is probably more misinformation about sport psychology than any of the sport sciences which aim to aid the performer. However, everyone seems to recognise the importance of the mental state with phrases like 'psych out' forming a part of our sporting vocabulary. It seems foolish, therefore, not to consider the mental side along with all other aspects of your game. But first, a few general points about mental training.

The most effective type of mental training involves the learning of various skills which can be put into practice at the appropriate moment. Just like physical skills these techniques take time to learn (some more than others) and need to be practised regularly. In addition, just like squash strokes, some will come easily and be used frequently while others are saved for that special occasion. Developing a full repertoire is important, though, if you do not want to get caught out.

Of course, mental training can be used to help a player who has a particular problem such as a slump in performance. This sort of crisis management is less effective, however, and is rather like starting your training two weeks before a marathon. Every little helps but short-term improvements are pretty small. A mental-training programme should therefore form a part of your on-going development as a player. Just as with your physical fitness all aspects are inter-related and developing a balance is essential. To make things clearer, the various mental components are considered in the situations in which they are most useful.

PRE-MATCH SKILLS

Arousal Effects and How to Control Them

Whenever the body is placed under pressure it reacts by getting ready to cope. The same is true of both physical pressure and mental pressure, or stress as it is usually called, and in fact any sort of stress will result in both physical and mental 'get ready' responses. The physical effects of stress are usually called arousal and all players at whatever level have experienced one or more of the symptoms. Particularly common are butterflies in the stomach, sweating and aching muscles. The mental effects are less apparent but just as common. Of course, to perform

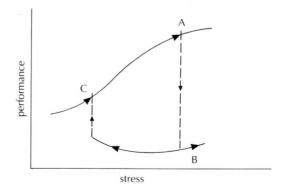

Fig 57   The catastrophe curve relationship between arousal and performance.

...ell in squash you must be worked up to some degree, and it is too much stress that seems to cause problems. This is shown well in Fig 57. The best performance will usually occur when the player is subjected to medium levels of stress.

As the diagram shows, the player must be worked up in order to produce his best. This occurs at the stage marked A. Any further increase in stress will result in a rapid drop in performance – the player cracks under pressure, as will be evident from his game. (This is shown as B.) To regain his normal level of play the person must lower his arousal level and try to stop worrying. Only when he is fairly relaxed will he be able to perform effectively (point C on the diagram). Because of the sudden drop in performance which occurs, this graph is called the 'catastrophe curve' and you may well have experienced this effect in your play.

From this you can see that at least two mental techniques are required, one to increase arousal levels and one to lower them. Since overarousal is more common than underarousal we will consider the lowering techniques first.

Relaxation and Tension-Control Techniques

There are many different mental techniques available to the athlete and detailed descriptions will be found in the books listed in the Further Reading section. At a later stage in your mental-skills training, you may wish to try other approaches but a very common and effective technique, progressive muscle relaxation (PMR), is an excellent first step. Originally developed in the 1930s by Edmund Jacobson, PMR forms the basis of many mental-skills programmes used in medicine, health education and sport. The idea behind PMR is that, as a result of practice, you can learn to recognise and eliminate tension in the body, eventually in a few seconds. This may explain why in the early stages you learn to relax by making your muscles as tight as possible. Any relaxation procedure may carry slight risks for certain individuals, for example, those with circulatory problems or on long-term medication. If in doubt, check with your doctor before starting.

Relaxation Procedures

These procedures should be practised twice a day for about ten minutes at a time (evenings are often a good time to practise). The order of steps involved is very important; however, the particular words or thoughts that the athlete uses to accomplish each step are not. When you are concentrating on relaxing your arms, you can say anything: 'Now I'm going to release all the muscular tension in my hands, fingers and forearms,' or 'Now I'm going to relax the muscles in my hands, fingers and arms.'

Prior to beginning the exercise, find a quiet, comfortable place where you will not be disturbed and where you can either sit or lie down. If you wear contact lenses, you may want to remove them. If you have on restrictive clothing (like a tie), you may want to loosen it. Make yourself comfortable with your hands at your sides or in your lap and you are ready to begin.

(i) Close your eyes and take three deep breaths, inhaling and exhaling deeply and slowly. As you exhale, relax your entire body as much as you can. Continue to notice your breathing throughout the session. You will find that as you exhale, your relaxation will become deeper.

(ii) Now clench both of your fists. Close them and squeeze them tighter and tighter together. As you squeeze them, notice the tension in your forearms, your hands and your fingers. That is fine. Now let them go and relax them. Let your fingers become loose and notice the pleasant feeling of

One of the most exciting players to watch and one of the Australian
World Champion team in 1989 – Rodney Martin.

heaviness in your arms and hands as the tension disappears. Feel the heaviness of your arms and hands as they rest against your body or the chair. That is fine. Try it one more time; clench both fists and feel the tension, squeeze harder, hold the tension, now let go and completely relax.

(iii) Now bend your elbows, clench your fists and flex your biceps. Flex them harder, hold the tension and study it. Now unbend your elbows, relax your hands, get your arms back into a comfortable position, study how your arms feel as you completely let go and relax them.

(iv) Now straighten your arms and flex the triceps muscle in the back of your upper arms. Hold the tension, increase it, squeeze harder, study the tension. That is fine. Now relax, return your arms to a comfortable position and enjoy the release from the tension. Enjoy the feelings, and even when you feel completely relaxed, try to let go even more.

(v) Now clench your teeth, feel the muscles tightening in your neck and jaws. Once again, study the tension, clench your teeth tighter and tighter. Now relax your jaws, let your mouth open slightly, and feel your muscles loosen, feel the relief from the tension.

(vi) Pay attention to your neck muscles. Press your head back as far as it will go and feel the tension, now roll it straight to the right. Again feel the increase in the tension in your muscles. Move your head to the left, pressing hard and feeling the tension in your muscles; hold the same position and study the tension. Now let your head move into a comfortable position and relax the muscles in your neck and shoulders. Notice the pleasant change as you feel the tension leaving your muscles. Pay attention to how your neck and shoulders feel when the muscles are relaxed.

(vii) Now pay attention to your breathing and relax your entire body. Breathe deeply and slowly, and as you exhale, relax all the muscles in your arms. Just let yourself go and completely relax. Let your mouth open slightly and relax the muscles in your face, jaw and forehead. Relax the muscles in your neck and shoulders . . . relax the muscles in your feet, your calves, and your thighs . . . that is fine . . . just completely relax and let yourself go. Continue to breathe deeply and slowly, and enjoy the pleasant feeling of being completely relaxed.

(viii) Now since you have relaxed so completely, it is best to take your time in moving around. Get out of this relaxed state by using three steps. First, count one and take a deep breath and hold it. Second, count two and stretch your arms and legs, then exhale. Third, count three and open your eyes. You should be wide awake and feeling very relaxed and comfortable.

Procedure Summary

(i) Close your eyes and breathe deeply and slowly.

(ii) Relax the muscles in your forearms.

(iii) Relax your biceps.

(iv) Relax your triceps.

(v) Relax your face, jaw and forehead.

(vi) Relax your neck and shoulders.

(vii) Breathe slowly and relax your entire body.

(viii) Take a deep breath, stretch, and open your eyes.

These relaxation procedures are reprinted with permission from R. M. Nideffer, *The Inner Athlete* (Thomas Y. Crowell, 1976). Exercises for PMR are shown in Fig 58.

As you improve in your ability to discriminate between tension and relaxation, the tensing part of the procedure can be cut and muscle groups combined. Eventually the whole procedure will be quite short and you will be ready to use it in a competitive situation. It can be used whenever you feel over-

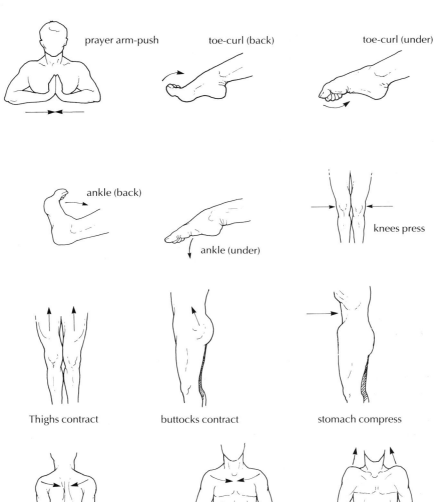

prayer arm-push   toe-curl (back)   toe-curl (under)

ankle (back)

ankle (under)

knees press

Thighs contract   buttocks contract   stomach compress

shoulder blades (back)   shoulder blades (forward)   shoulder blades (up)

shoulders down-reach   chin compress on to neck   press head on to mat

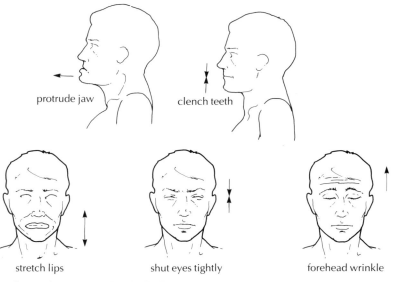

Fig 58   Exercises for tension recognition in PMR.

anxious, whether this is two days or two hours before the match. Your practice will be much easier if you make a tape of the instructions, delivered at a suitable speed and with gaps in which you can obey the instruction. A very good series of ready-made tapes which cover all the various stages of PMR are available from the National Coaching Foundation or the Scottish Sports Council – both the addresses are provided at the back of the book.

Mental Imagery

Imagery is an extremely useful mental skill which has a wide variety of uses. You have probably used imagery techniques already and not even realised it. The link between mind and body is apparent in many ordinary situations. If you are hungry, for example, imagining your favourite food will result in a physical response – your mouth waters. Watching a game may also result in various 'twitches' as you imagine yourself participating; test it yourself the next time you watch a

close race finish or squash game. The problem comes when you try to control the images or produce them at will. Some people find this easier than others, but everyone benefits from regular practice of the skill before it is used in a competitive situation. Try to picture yourself in a favourite place, say on the beach or performing a well-known skill like peeling an orange.

The following suggestions may be helpful. To start with, get as relaxed as possible, ensuring that there will be no distracting noises to interfere with your mental picture. When you have relaxed, start to build up the scene in your mind adding or paying attention to more and more detail as and when you are ready. Try to incorporate all your senses to make the scene more vivid. Notice the sound of the sea and the sand between your toes or the smell and stickiness of the orange. If there is movement in your image ensure it happens at normal speed; try to avoid the slow-motion action replay. Short, frequent practice sessions are best in the early stages, therefore after a reasonable time leave your image by 'switching it off' or returning along the path which you used to enter the situation. After this, use the same procedure which you learned for PMR. Use the mental imagery questionnaire in Fig 59 to assess your performance. Remember that you will get better with practice. If you find the image a problem to control, you can use a tape recording of the various aspects in your image to jog your memory.

When you are satisfied with your performance on the 'neutral' image, try a sport-specific setting. You might, in your mind's eye, change into your kit, walk on to the court and run through a few shots. Monitor your performance as before. Finally, start to use your new-found skill effectively by incorporating it into your pre-match preparation. You may have noticed the calming influence of relaxing pictures in your PMR sessions – these can be used to calm your mind in the time before the game. Remember to allow sufficient time to return from your relaxing scene or your early play may suffer. To avoid this problem, take heed to the next section.

Psyching-up

As you can see from the catastrophe curve presented in Fig 57, not enough arousal can be as problematic as too much. If you view the approaching game with little concern you are unlikely to produce your best play and will probably start slowly. Finding yourself one game down against a weaker opponent will, of course, induce a rapid rise in arousal but by then it may be too late. It is all a case of what you make yourself think. The diagram in Fig 60 explains the problem.

If you think that your opponent is very weak, you may be bored at the prospect of the game. Conversely, a game against Jansher Khan is likely to be a great worry. A game in which you feel that you are evenly matched

		TICK ONE	
	Yes	**In Between**	**No**
(i) Could you 'see' and 'feel' yourself perform the skill?			
(ii) Could you control the picture?			
(iii) Was the picture clear?			
(iv) Was the skill executed successfully?			
(v) Was the skill at normal speed?			
(vi) Did you stay relaxed?			
(vii) Did you stay alert?			
(viii) Did you use senses other than just 'sight' and 'feel'?			

Fig 59 Mental imagery questionnaire. Answer the questions after each of your initial training sessions with mental imagery. This is based on work by Lew Hardy and John Fazey in The Coach at Work (National Coaching Foundation, 1986).

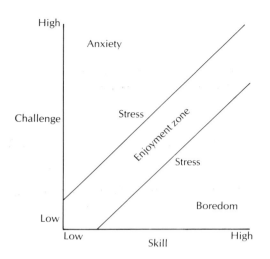

Fig 60   Optimal enjoyment through matching challenge and skill, adapted from Csikszentmihalyi, M., Beyond Boredom and Anxiety (Jossey-Bass, 1975).

is likely to produce your best play and the most enjoyment.

These problems can be overcome in two ways, both of which should be incorporated into your pre-match routine. Firstly, your thoughts and actions should focus on factors within your control, i.e. you, not your opponent. Use PMR together with relaxing images until the time comes for you to start your build-up. Physical warm-ups and stroke play can be used together with the imagery of yourself performing well. Concentrate on your own game plan, what you have to do. Secondly, focus throughout on goals which you have previously decided for the match. These skills will be discussed in detail later in the chapter but for the moment recognise that you can manipulate the challenge of the game by setting yourself a realistic target. In practice games against weaker players you can work on facets of your play. With a stronger player you need to recognise that taking four points in a game may be a good performance for you.

Your psych-up is like your physical warm-up, designed to get you to the start of the game and ready to produce your best. Just as the physical demands are built up to game pace, so your mental warm-up should be designed to build you up gradually to the optimum state. Imagery can be used in this way and some athletes combine it with music to develop the right attitude. The themes from *Chariots of Fire* and *Rocky* are often used to psych up. Working to develop a consistent and effective routine is as important as practising your strokes. Experiment a little and when you have a routine, use it in all matches.

DURING THE COMPETITION

Concentration and Attention Control

During your practice of relaxation or imagery, you may well have found that thoughts just seemed to appear in your head. Alternatively your image, relaxing or otherwise, may have faded. If so, you will have realised just how hard it is to concentrate while eliminating negative or irrelevant thoughts. In squash the pressure situation is often an occasion for the mind to wander, frequently with disastrous results. Concentration is therefore a really important mental skill. The ability to concentrate and dismiss distractions is common in top players but can this ability be learnt? The good news is it can but, as before, this requires practice. An examination of the nature of concentration will help you to understand the processes and problems involved.

Concentration can be best thought of as the ability to pay attention to the right things at the right time. In a squash game there is a great deal going on, only some of which is relevant. The good 'concentrator' must be able to do two things: know what to look at and be able to focus on that and nothing else.

Of course, knowing what to look for may be quite complicated: trying to read your opponent's game requires you to pay a great deal of attention to many things. The diagram in Fig 61 explains this quite nicely. It is based on the work of an American Sport Psychologist, Robert Nideffer, who suggested that attentional focus (what you pay attention to) can be classified as internal or external (i.e. things inside or outside the body) and broad or narrow (i.e. lots of things or very few). As the diagram shows, each of these different ways of paying attention is suited to a particular facet of squash. In other words, you must practise to develop all the ways of paying attention and learn to switch from one to the other as the situation demands.

Training to concentrate is quite difficult, but a variety of simple drills can be used to make a start. You could try to perform some difficult mental arithmetic or do a crossword in the rest intervals of a hard training session. Another idea would be to try playing while others try to distract you. This technique is particularly useful for preparing you to cope with playing before a crowd or on a glass court. At a later stage your opponent in practice games could start to do the things which you find most distracting – arguing with the referee or taking a long time to serve, for example. Make sure that you know about it in advance or things might get nasty. The main thing is to make sure that you know what you should be paying attention to – consult your coach and learn to watch opponents for clues to their next move.

Between Matches

The intervals between games and matches can be a watershed for you or your opponent. Used properly, time off-court can provide a calming period together with a chance to review and replan your play under less pressured conditions. All too often, however, the break in your rhythm leads to a loss

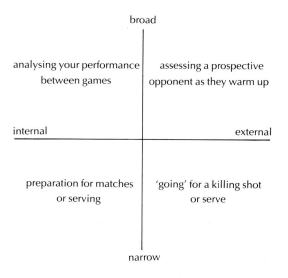

Fig 61   Differing types of attention in squash.

of focus and a slow start next time. This is even worse when you are losing, the constant brooding on your mistakes may produce a bout of depression or 'here I go again' feelings from which it is almost impossible to recover.

To make the best use of breaks in play you must develop a procedure which maintains your focus whilst preventing the negative thoughts which are so easy to generate. The procedure will depend on the break's length. Between games, in the ninety seconds allowed, you can quickly analyse your performance, focus on the things which *you* did or needed to do and run through them by use of mental imagery. The personal focus is essential. In spite of the commonly held beliefs in 'psyching out' your opponent, you really cannot do anything about his performance. Concentrate on what you need to do and leave him to worry or lose concentration all by himself. Equally vital is to avoid negative self-criticism. Cursing yourself for missing that last point is totally useless but all too common. Gallwey's book *The Inner*

Game of Tennis makes some interesting points on the tendency which we all have to abuse ourselves. Use the quick burst relaxation technique outlined earlier and rephrase your self-talk to emphasise what you must do. So, 'Collins you idiot, you threw that game away' becomes 'Stay calm, just keep a good line and wait for them to make a mistake'. If you have a longer break between matches, in a tournament situation for example, you should review your performance positively, then relax until the time comes for you to warm up for the next match. In this way much nervous and physical energy is saved for on court. You must, of course, know how long your warm-up takes – yet another reason for developing a system.

MAKING THE MOST OF YOUR TRAINING

Self-confidence and Goal Setting

Mentally speaking, the main aim of your training programme is that when you walk on court for a game you feel as prepared as you possibly could be. The crucial word here is feel. Your perception of how ready you are is usually called self-confidence and building self-confidence is an important consideration in your training. Research has shown that your self-confidence is improved most effectively by actual achievements. This is one big reason for the advantage that more experienced performers usually have. Another important consideration is how you feel about the weaknesses in your game. All too often players try to forget their weaknesses and never work on them in training. As a consequence, the weakness gets built up in the player's mind and the worry that results gets in the way of the brain activity necessary to control the movement. This leads to more worry and the downward spiral that can wreck a player's career or at least prevent him from realising his full potential. What is needed, therefore, is a technique which provides plenty of achievement in training while ensuring that the weak points of your game are confronted and strengthened. Such a technique, imported from the world of business, is called goal setting.

Most top-level performers, in any activity, plan their preparation with great care. Goal setting is a formalised way of doing this and enables you to keep a close eye on your progress. It works like this. First of all you decide on your long-term aims or targets within the game. These must be positive, measurable and within your control; the various aims will usually be linked in some way and will be based on a review of your current strengths and weaknesses. An example set of goals is shown in Fig 62. Notice that the first

Long-term goals	Goals for next month	Goals for next week
To get into the top five of the club's senior 'ladder'.	To play at least three matches per week.	Make court bookings for next week now.
	To improve the consistency of my forehand and backhand drives so that I can maintain a rally of at least thirty shots.	(i) To complete at least two, fifteen minute practice sessions on the drive. (ii) Achieve a 9/10 score on pairs practice #6 (see Chapter 1).
To gain a place on the club team.	To play practice games against two of the club team members.	Watch one club team match and complete a brief analysis of the no. 5 player's game.

Fig 62 Examples of long-term, intermediate and short-term goals.

one is the basis for the rest, i.e. if you want to do this then you will have to be able to do this.

Your coach or playing partners may help you to arrive at these goals but you can manage by yourself if you make a realistic assessment of your current level. All the goals satisfy the criteria given above: they are positive, measurable and depend on you doing things (i.e. are within your control). Deciding which goals to follow will force you to make some important decisions such as, 'What do I want from the game?', 'How much time am I prepared to give each week?' This is, in itself, a useful exercise.

Having decided on your long-term goals, you must now plan a series of steps towards achieving them. Doing this will require you to allocate time to each facet of your training so that the right balance is maintained. Goals can be set monthly or weekly but using both together is most effective. The short-term goals are very specific and provide you with exactly what you should be doing in each training session. This helps to focus your mind on the job at hand, your practice time becomes more purposeful and efficient. Regular reassessment of your progress and adapting your goals will keep your efforts tuned to the optimum level.

Going through the goal-setting process will ensure that the weak aspects of your game are identified and receive plenty of remedial attention. We all tend to like working on things we are good at. Goals may, however, lay down a number of repetitions which we must attempt – persistence and therefore progress is improved. If your goals are set at the right level you will also get plenty of achievement. Pitching these targets at the right level takes a bit of practice. If they are too easy you will get bored, too hard and you will give up. Once you get this right you can make the goals important by rewarding yourself for each intermediate goal you reach.

Making the Most of Your Coach

Some players are lucky enough to have the services of a personal coach, while others may take lessons from a professional every so often. The vast majority, however, have to depend on their fellow players for advice on their play, both during a match and in practice. In all these cases, making the most of the information is a definite skill and deserves some consideration in your mental-training programme. Advice from an observer, who we will presume knows what he is talking about, must be used in different ways, depending on the circumstances.

In practice, the pressure is of a low intensity and you can afford to discuss the suggestions and take your time in implementing them. Indeed unless the suggestions are very minor you will have to take your time. Consideration of how you control your movements will demonstrate this. When you perform a skill which you know well, walking for example, the amount of 'conscious thinking space' required to control the movement is relatively small. This has two advantages: you have plenty of space left to think about other things and the performance of the skill is very smooth and efficient. This sort of control is also essential for your play in squash. If someone suggests a modification, however, you have to think more about the skill – therefore you have less space to think about the game, and poorer timing since the 'conscious control' is slower and less efficient. A great deal of time-consuming practice is needed to develop a new 'motor programme' (the set of instructions which your brain uses to control the movement). Even when the new programme is established, the old way of doing things is still likely to crop up, especially in pressure situations. You must practise the new skill in a variety of situations, including game play, until its use is totally automatic.

So if someone suggests a change in style or

Mark Maclean playing short from in front of his opponent – Brian Beeson.

a new technique you must consider the pros and cons carefully. Do you have the time to learn the new skill thoroughly? Can you put in enough practice at the new skill to establish it as the strongest programme? Will the change give you a significant improvement? If not, perhaps you should abandon the idea or at least delay change until the off season. So the short answer is treat advice with care, do not chop and change your playing style without considering the consequences.

Between games, the situation is obviously more pressured and, while the advice above still applies, you will not be able to consider such major changes. Unfortunately, there always seems to be one of your team or another expert about who thinks that you can. The problem is, once again, linked to the thinking space available. Imagine the situation: you have ninety seconds, you are tired and trying hard to concentrate on your game without (as advised earlier) abusing yourself for mistakes. The amount of space available is very low and you can consider only a few points. The coaching between games, therefore, must provide two or three points only – things which you must do stated in positive terms. Long preambles or detailed advice on your backhand just will not work. If you watch boxing or basketball on television you will see some good examples of how to do this. So remember, state a few points in positive terms and do not discuss the mistakes in the last game, save that for later.

PUTTING IT ALL TOGETHER

You may have noticed that the different sections above seem to overlap, with similar skills and advice appearing for different applications. This is deliberate; the information provided will ensure you have a comprehensive, practical and usable package of skills provided that you practise regularly. A wide variety of mental skills does exist but they are all designed to do one job – to enable you to adjust your level of activation and your thoughts to those most appropriate to the demands of the situation. Deciding on what is appropriate obviously needs some thought but the theory included in the chapter should help you to reach decisions based on actual facts. One big factor to recognise is that you can improve the mental aspect of your game, in the same way that other aspects are developed, i.e. by regular and progressive practice. If you decide to incorporate mental skills training into your programme, make sure that the skills are effective in training before you try to use them in a game. Start with PMR, then begin to experiment with imagery. Goal setting should also be incorporated relatively early on. Further applications and advice on developing your mental skills are provided in the books listed in the Further Reading section.

6 Summary and Programme Planning

In this book we have attempted to provide information on all the facets of performance which need to be considered in a training programme. Your first reaction may be to give up work and your social life in order for you to be able to fit everything in. Unfortunately this is not realistic so, as was mentioned earlier, any training programme tends to be a compromise which best suits the particular needs of the individual. To do this effectively, base your programme on a realistic appraisal of your current level, strengths/weaknesses and time available. This is, perhaps, easier said than done but the more attention which

This close encounter may well need the referees decision.

you pay to this stage, the more effective your eventual programme will be.

In many sports, the year is split up into sections or periods to facilitate the planning. This training cycle can be very complex but basically consists of general preparation, a pre-season phase, in season/competition and a post-season recovery period. Of course, most squash players have no season as such but just continue to play all year round. If you are a top-class player on the pro circuit, a careful build-up is necessary to arrive at tournaments in optimum condition. This is a specialised job and is beyond the scope of this book. However, some sort of phasing in training is useful since working on the same things continuously can get very boring. Indeed, constant hard training can become counterproductive; progress becomes impossible and injury may result. Based on your own personal assessment, therefore, design a yearly programme which emphasises different aspects at different times. At a general level this is perfectly satisfactory as long as you remember a few important points:

(i) Make sure your training is progressive, i.e. necessary preparatory work is completed (e.g. strength before power, aerobic before anaerobic, basic drive before boasts, and so on).

(ii) Allow yourself some rest or recovery time away from squash training. Even the keenest player can get turned off by too intense a schedule. A different sport or activity will enable you to return to training with renewed vigour.

(iii) It is human nature to do most of what we enjoy and avoid what we do not. Make sure that your programme spends most time on your weaknesses, not your strengths.

In conclusion, it must be emphasised that each individual must personalise his training towards his own aims and within the limitations of his own circumstances. Good use of the information provided here should enable any player to fulfil his own goals with consequent fulfilment and satisfaction. We hope you enjoy yourselves.

Glossary

Aerobic 'With oxygen'; used to describe 'steady-state' exercise where the body relies on oxygen as a continuous source of fuel.

Amenorrhoea Absence of normal female monthly cycles or periods.

Amino acid The constituent parts of protein: eight of these acids cannot be made in the body (these are termed essential) and must form part of our diet. Another twelve can be synthesised in the body.

Anaemia A deficiency of red blood cells, or of their haemoglobin. Most likely to occur in women with heavy periods or otherwise due to insufficient iron replacement.

Basal Metabolic Rate (BMR) A term used to describe the absolute amount of energy required to maintain the body function for life. It is a very precise measure made when the subject is awake, at perfect rest, 12 hours after a meal and in a thermoneutral environment.

Boast Shot played to hit the side or back wall before reaching the front wall.

Body Mass Index (BMI) A convenient way to express the ratio of height to weight and give a simple estimate of abnormal weight for height. BMI is weight (kilograms) divided by the height (metres) squared and should lie in the range 17–25.

Caffeine A drug found in tea, coffee, chocolate and some carbonated beverages. Promotes fatty acid release, affects the cardiovascular system and is a diuretic.

Calorie A very small, precisely defined unit of heat. One thousand calories are equivalent to one kilocalorie or kcal.

Carbohydrates Molecules containing carbon, hydrogen and oxygen. They may be small simple units, often sweet, such as glucose, sucrose or larger units, often taste-less, such as starch. We cannot digest all carbohydrates and some are termed 'unavailable'; these include cellulose (dietary fibre). Carbohydrates provide energy for the body, about 4 kcals per gram or 120kcal per oz.

Cardiorespiratory exercise Exercise such as running, cycling, swimming, or any exercise utilising large muscle groups for an extended period of time; develops the ability of the blood, heart, lungs and other systems of the body to persist in work.

Cool-down A period of light exercise and stretching after vigorous activity.

Cut Applied to the ball when the swing starts high and the racket cuts across the back of the ball, bringing it sharply downwards.

Dehydration Loss of body fluid with inadequate replacement. Liable to result from excessive sweating, diarrhoea or vomiting.

Dietary deficiency Inadequate intake of an essential nutrient which results in reduced body stores of the nutrient and eventually affects the body function. Diagnosis of a deficiency requires biochemical tests.

Dietary fibre That part of our food which is not digested by our normal digestive juices and therefore remains in the intestine providing bulk. However, dietary fibre is largely digested by organisms in the large bowel and as such can be absorbed to provide energy.

Dislocation A displacement of the bony surfaces at a joint so that the ends of the bones do not meet, or meet incorrectly. Requires immediate referral to a doctor.

Doping The use of substances which artificially improve or augment an athlete's performance.

Drop Short shot aimed to finish close to the front wall.

Fats Molecules containing carbon, hydrogen and oxygen. The small molecules are called fatty acids and dietary fats are a mixture of different fatty acids often held together by another molecule of glycerol and are then referred to simply as fat. Fats provide energy, 9kcal per g or 270kcal per oz.

Flexibility A component of physical fitness or form of exercise which refers to the stretching of muscles.

Glycogen The form in which the mammalian body stores carbohydrate. It is mainly stored in the liver and muscles and constitutes a very mobile but limited store of energy for the body. It can be used without the presence of oxygen, i.e. anaerobically.

Haemoglobin The oxygen-carrying component of red blood cells composed of an iron-based substance.

Isokinetic A form of resistance training where a machine provides resistance which allows for constant limb speed.

Isometric A form of resistance training where no movement takes place.

Isotonic A form of resistance training involving the lifting of free-standing objects, such as barbells.

Joule A very small and precise measure of the amount of work. The energy in food is related to the amount of work it can generate and therefore sometimes the energy value of food is expressed in joules. One thousand joules form one kilojoule or kJ. One kcal is equivalent to 4.2 kJ.

Ligaments Strong bands of fibrous tissue which bind bones together at a joint.

Lob High, slow shot played to drop into the back corner.

Mental imagery The process of practising a skill in the mind rather than through physical practice.

Minerals Inert substances some of which are essential to the body for its functioning. Calcium, magnesium, sodium, potassium, phosphorous, iron and zinc are some of these essential minerals.

Muscular endurance The ability to contract a muscle, or group of muscles, continuously over time.

Nick The join between the side wall and the floor. When the ball hits the nick it cannot usually be returned.

Nutrients Those parts of food which are used by the body to allow functioning of cells. Carbohydrates and fats are 'burned' to provide energy for cells to work – internally in order to make more tissue, for example, and externally to propel the body. Protein, vitamins and minerals are all used by the cells to function normally.

Open racket face When the racket face hits the ball with the top edge of the racket head behind the lower edge. This makes the ball spin, lose speed and rise.

Osteoarthritis The surfaces of bones at a joint are covered in cartilage which may become worn away, particularly in a joint which has been previously damaged. The joint may be painful, swollen, or stiff.

Osteoporosis A condition, mainly in women, in which the bones become increasingly thin and brittle – it is caused by reduced sex hormones and possibly low intake of calcium.

Overload System in which training is progressively increased.

Power The combination of strength and speed.

Progressive Muscular Relaxation (PMR) A form of relaxation training which teaches the recognition of tension and relaxation through a series of muscle-tension exercises.

Proprioceptive Neuromuscular Facilitation (PNF) A form of flexibility training which requires the muscle to be contracted before stretching.

Protein The part of food that contains amino acids. It can be used for energy and provides 4kcal per g or 120kcal per oz.

Rally A number of consecutive shots, played either by one player or two players hitting the ball alternately.

Reaction time The time which elapses between the stimulus and the start of the movement in response to the stimulus.

Service Shot played to start the game off.

Skinfold thickness The layer of body fat lying directly beneath the skin which can be measured using skinfold callipers. This layer of fat is related to total body fat which may be estimated from this method.

Sorbothane A synthetic substance which absorbs energy well and is used as a 'shock-absorber' for inserts into shoes, mainly at the heel.

Sports anaemia Probably not true anaemia; the increase in plasma volume brought on by a serious training schedule dilutes the red cells reducing their concentration, the total number of red cells remaining the same.

Sprain An injury to the ligaments around a joint which may produce pain, swelling and discolouration.

Shake hands grip Standard grip for all strokes, attained by shaking hands with the handle when the racket head is vertical. Fingers should be slightly spread and the 'V' between first finger and thumb should line up with the left hand corner of the shaft.

Strength The ability of the muscle to exert force.

Stress fracture A minute crack in the bone due to repeated overloading by inappropriately rapid increase in training loads.

Tendon White 'cords' which attach muscles to the bones. They may become inflamed (tendonitis), partially torn, or completely broken (ruptured tendon).

Tonicity of fluid The concentration of particles in a solution compared to the concentration of particles in body fluids, especially blood. If the concentration in a solution is greater than blood it is termed hypertonic; if lower in concentration, hypotonic. Water will always travel from a less concentrated solution to a more concentrated solution.

Variable resistance training A form of resistance training which varies the loading to accommodate the mechanical efficiency of body levers so the optimal tension is placed on the muscle throughout the whole range of movement.

Vitamins Molecules which are found in food and are essential to cells for their efficient functioning. Some vitamins are associated and soluble in fat (A, D, E, K), others are soluble in water (B and C).

Volley When the ball is struck before it bounces on the floor.

Warm-up Light, mainly aerobic and flexibility exercises prior to vigorous activity.

Further Reading

Game Skills

Chapman, C., Lincoln, B., Poynder, J. and Wright, P., *SRA/WSRA Guide to Better Squash* (Pan, 1989)

Chapman, C. and Richardson, J., *250 Practices for Squash Players* (SRA)

Martin, G. and Wallace, H., *Squash: A New Approach* (A & C Black, 1984)

Taylor, J., *Squash* (Pelham Books, 1985)

Mental Training

Harris, D. V. & Harris, B. L., *The Athletes Guide to Sport Psychology: Mental Skills for Physical People* (Leisure Press, 1984)

Orlick, T., *In Pursuit of Excellence* (Human Kinetics, 1980)

National Coaching Foundation, *The Coach at Work* (1986)

Sports Injuries

Grisogono, V., *Sports Injuries: a Self-help Guide* (John Murray, 1984)

National Coaching Foundation, *Safety First for Coaches* (1986)

Read, M. and Wade, P., *Sports and Medicine* (Butterworth, 1981)

St John Ambulance, *First Aid Manual* (Dorling Kindersley, 1982)

Physical Fitness

Anderson, B., *Stretching* (Pelham, 1980)

Fox, E., *Sports Physiology* (Saunders College, 1979)

Hazeldine, R., *Fitness for Sport* (The Crowood Press, 1985)

Lear, P. J., *Weight Training* (A & C Black, 1988)

National Coaching Foundation, *Physiology and Performance* (1986)

National Strength and Conditioning Association Journal

Nutrition

DHSS, *Recommended Amounts of Food Energy and Nutrients for Groups of People in the UK* (Report on Health and Social Subjects No. 15, 1979)

Eisenmann, P. and Johnson D., *Coaches' Guide to Nutrition and Weight Control* (Human Kinetics, 1982)

Haskell, W. *et al.*, *Nutrition and Athletic Performance* (Bull Publishing, 1982)

Ministry of Agriculture, Fisheries and Food, Manual of Nutrition (HMSO, 1985)

Paul, A. and Southgate, D., *McCance and Widdowson's 'The Composition of Foods'* (HMSO, 1978)

Useful Addresses

British Amateur Weight Lifters' Association, 3 Iffley Turn, Oxford OX4 4DY.

British Association of Sports Sciences, c/o National Coaching Foundation (*see* below).

National Coaching Foundation, 4 College Close, Beckett Park, Leeds LS6 3QH.

Scottish Sports Council, 1 St. Colme Street, Edinburgh EH3 6AA.

Sports Council, 16 Upper Woburn Place, London WC1H 0QP.

St John Ambulance, Supplies Department, Priory House, St John's Gate, Clerkenwell, London EC1M 4DA.

Squash Rackets Association, WestPoint, 33/34 Warple Way, London W3 0RQ.

Welsh Squash Rackets Federation, 7 Kymin Terrace, Penarth, Cardiff CF6 1AP.

Scottish Squash Rackets Association, Caledonia House, South Gyle, Edinburgh EH12 9DQ.

Irish Squash Rackets Association, Irish Womens SRA, House of Sport, Long Mile Road, Dublin 12.

ISRF, 82 Cathedral Road, Cardiff CF1 9PG.

Index